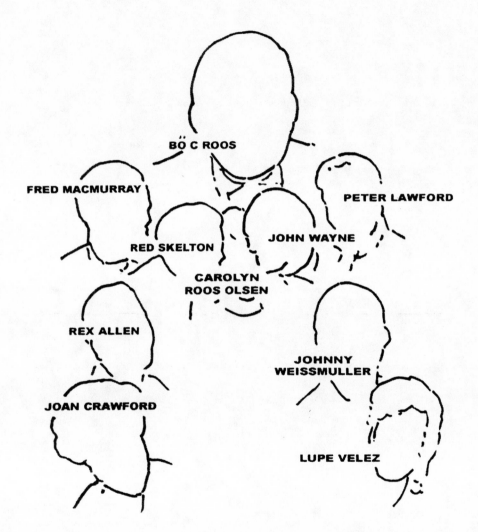

HOLLYWOOD'S
MAN WHO WORRIED FOR THE STARS

THE STORY OF BÖ ROOS

by

Carolyn Roos Olsen

with

Marylin Hudson

**Business Manager for
100+ Stars**

authorHOUSE®

AuthorHouse™
1663 Liberty Drive, Suite 200
Bloomington, IN 47403
www.authorhouse.com
Phone: 1-800-839-8640

First published by AuthorHouse 4/25/2008

ISBN: 978-1-4343-5114-2 (sc)
ISBN: 978-1-4343-5113-5 (hc)

Library of Congress Control Number: 2007909485

Printed in the United States of America
Bloomington, Indiana

This book is printed on acid-free paper.

TABLE OF CONTENTS

PROLOGUE

REMEMBERING MY FATHER

Orson Welles once said that my father, Bö Christian Roos, was becoming more famous than some of his clients. Since his clients included the likes of John Wayne, Red Skelton, Fred MacMurray, Johnny Weissmuller, *and* Orson Welles, plus Marlene Dietrich, Joan Crawford, James Arness, Howard Keel, and many more, that was quite a statement.

Edward R. Murrow interviewed my father on his television show. The *Saturday Evening Post*, *Cosmopolitan*, the *New York Times, Liberty* magazine, *Daily Variety*, the *Hollywood Reporter,* and local newspapers regularly ran stories about him, as did publications overseas and, in particular, Mexico. Gossip columnists from Louella Parsons to Hedda Hopper wrote about him in their syndicated columns. To them and their viewers and readers, he was newsworthy.

To his clients and the press he was "Mr. Deductible," "The Man Who Worried for the Stars," and "a legend in his own time." Dad was considered a pioneer and an innovator in financial management. He was one of the first Hollywood business managers, starting his business in the early 1930s and going until the mid-1960s, helping clients who segued from silents to talkies, vaudeville to radio, stage to film, and film to television. It was fascinating to watch his mind work as he wheeled and dealed, strategized with agents, and negotiated with studios, networks, stage producers, and many others, always with the goal in mind of maximizing the money his clients could earn and retain.

He was a colorful, vibrant man to be around. His friendships stretched around the world and included presidents, diplomats, princes, business tycoons, a Queen and a King, all of whom spilled over into his personal as well as professional life.

For us, his family, he created a world of excitement, whether it was at home or on his boat in Catalina or at a nightclub in Hollywood or on a trip to Hawaii, Acapulco, London, Paris, New York, or Rome.

I became his secretary in the 1940s and was privy to his activities and worked with him on and off through the years. Even back then people said, "Somebody should write a book about Bö Roos." Others said, "You *can't* write a book; nobody would believe it." I thought it was a good idea, but marriage, raising three children, and being Public Relations manager for the Monsanto Company in Disneyland for ten years, (VIPing their contacts from around the World), took up all my time until now.

Aside from wanting to leave a record for the family of a remarkable man, what motivated me to finally write it is my disappointment in some of the accounts written about him and about events I knew firsthand. Some are totally inaccurate as to facts; others are rehashes of previous material from sources who were not there. I'm sorry those few authors have painted the people I knew, loved, and worked with in such a negative cast now that they have passed on and can't defend themselves.

However, in looking back I realized the need to remember and verify many events and details from years ago. When my father's business, Beverly Management Corporation, closed its offices, I found that a great many irreplaceable files, including correspondence, photos, and records, had been lost along the way. However, I have scrapbooks, my own files, family records, and an enormous number of magazine and newspaper articles and interviews concerning my father. Many of the clippings are now yellowed and fragile. Quite a few don't include the writer, the publication, or the date, but whenever I could, I have given credit to the source. Many books have been used as references to check on events and especially dates.

It's been a marvelous experience, and I think Dad would have been pleased to have his story told.

Dad loved to get behind the wheel of the car for a Sunday outing. We never knew where we would end up.

ACKNOWLEDGMENTS

I would like to thank all the friends who encouraged me to write this book and all the authors who provided inspiration and advice.

Marylin Hudson took on the task of taking my material and experiences and helping me put it all into the kind of format that would best accomplish what I wanted in telling the story of my father, Bö Christian Roos, in the early motion picture industry..

Marylin's expertise in research and interest in that particular period of time in the motion picture industry was invaluable as we turned back time and relived that fascinating period in Hollywood history.

Many of my family members and friends, along with those who knew my father well, have contributed with some of their own memories, which I greatly appreciate.

Ideally, the many photographs I have included from my personal collection will help to enhance your feeling of that era from the 1930s through the 1960s.

Carolyn Roos Olsen

So After 50 Years . . . I Can Proudly Present Our Bö The Home Town Boy Who After These Many Years Of Struggle . . . Has Made His Voice Heard Around The World . . . So After These Few Words Of Praise And Admiration . . . I Now Give You The One And Only ——

MR. TELEPHONE *Shep*
OF 1953

This drawing was from the famous Wm. Wrigley Company's artist Otis Shephard and was presented to my Dad at the Century party. Dad regularly made at least sixty calls a day.

CHAPTER 1

WHAT A SWELL PARTY IT WAS

The "invitation" called it THE CENTURY PARTY, and some of the biggest and brightest of the Hollywood elite attended. The party was to celebrate the fiftieth birthdays of Bö Christian Roos and his director friend Bob Fellows. Society and motion picture columnist Cobina Wright reported that it was "a large scale party for over 600, capably handled by Bö Roos' charming daughter Carolyn."

The location was the Westside Tennis Club, owned by Bö Roos and several of his movie star clients. The bar of the club was decorated as an old-time saloon and included a barbershop quartet. The terrace, looking out over the pool and tennis courts, was turned into a northern Acapulco set with Mexican food and music. The large ballroom was made into a Cocoanut Grove scene with lush food being served, cocktails and wine flowing throughout, and music and dancing in the center.

What really makes a party is the guest list, and it was quite a stellar group; a "bluechip" collection of movie stars, directors, producers, writers, agents, business associates, family, and even a prince, a president, and an ambassador.

When Cole Porter came to Hollywood, he said people told him he'd be totally bored because nobody talked about anything but pictures. But after he was there awhile, he said, "I discovered I didn't want to talk about anything else myself."

Some of the guests at the Century Party in the Coconut Grove room set. (James Arness 'way in the back'.)

There was a lot of talk about movies; after all, that *was* our business. But there was much more. Our circle of friends, family, and clients had relationships that were interwoven like a crazy quilt over many years and stretched around the world. When we got together, there were many memories to share.

I'll try to re-create the scene, some fifty years after the fact. I can't remember everyone who was or wasn't there, but this is what it was like:

Giving the proceedings an international flair would be "P. B."—Prince Bernhard of the Netherlands, who took Dad elephant hunting in Africa; Sheik Ali Alireza,the future minister plenipotentiary of Saudi Arabia; Miguel Alemán, my dad's good friend and president of Mexico from 1946 to 1952; and Antonio Diaz Lombardo, the head of the Bank of Mexico. They would have a good time remembering the Mexican film festivals and how Dad earned his reputation as "The Aga Khan of Acapulco."

The singers might burst into song at any minute. Howard Keel had a lot to sing about—he'd have three films coming out in the next year alone: *Deep in My Heart*, *Rose Marie*, and *Seven Brides for Seven Brothers*. Kathryn Grayson, his costar in movies such as *Show Boat*, would probably be thinking about the future and the possibility of their touring together after the expected demise of the big film musicals. Jeannette MacDonald would reminisce about operettas, concerts, and Nelson Eddy.

Director J. Mitchell Leisen, Actress Ann Dvorak and Fred MacMurray's first wife, Lillian MacMurray.

Fred MacMurray with my Mom, Billie.

My husband Ted and I in the Northern Acapulco party set.

*John Wayne, surrounded as always by fans, with Harriet Parsons
to the far right and Frank Borzage lighting his pipe.*

*Character actor George Melville Cooper and wife, with
Frank Belcher, Director Frank Borzage and Dad.*

A whole contingent would have returned recently from location in Ireland on *The Quiet Man*, a film for which Dad helped put together the financing. John Ford had been the director, our client Andrew McLaglen was an assistant director, and Maureen O'Hara was the female lead. Ward Bond, who had been the priest/narrator in the film, would as always be razzing its star, John Wayne, his friend since college. They inevitably brought up and dramatized Ward's motorcycle accident and Dad's saving Ward's leg from amputation. When it came to career, Duke was on a roll, having been voted No. 1 on a poll of exhibitors every year from 1950 to 1953, partly because of his Oscar nomination for his role as Sergeant Stryker in *Sands of Iwo Jima* in 1949. Duke would soon buy out Bob Fellows's interest in their joint company and form Batjac, which would have a profound effect on Dad's business.

Both Duke and Dad would avoid the subject of Duke's messy, expensive, headline-making divorce from his second wife, the fireball Chata. It was a party, after all, so instead they'd talk about their great vacations in Mexico, their fishing trips and their boat the *Norwester*, and friends they'd made along the way.

In one corner, the British contingent would gather, including handsome Peter Lawford, who'd marry Patricia Kennedy the next year, initiating him into the Kennedy inner circle and making him a valued member of Sinatra's Rat Pack. There'd be several character actors whom you'd recognize from British drawing room comedies or films such as *Charge of the Light Brigade*. Joining them might be Bebe Daniels and Ben Lyon, who gave Dad his start among the film set back in the 1930s. They would reminisce about their years in England and tell stories about their World War II adventures. Ann Dvorak had driven an ambulance, and John Howard earned the Navy Cross and the French Croix de Guerre during the conflict.

I was glad to see that Rex Allen, the Arizona Cowboy, didn't bring his horse, who was often his sidekick, requiring special arrangements for oats and cleanup.

*Actor Patric Knowles showing our favorite
bartender, "Little Al", how to bartend.*

The Northern Acapulco set for the party.

*Bob Thom, Harriet Parsons, Bernard Newman, with Dad
and John Howard, enjoying the birthday festivities.*

Fred MacMurray, one of our dearest friends and our client forever, would be there even though he always looked as if he'd rather be on his ranch. He'd just finished *The Caine Mutiny* and would do a string of Disney movies, together with twelve years of *My Three Sons* on TV, all of which, plus his and Dad's investments, helped to make him one of the richest men in Hollywood.

Dear June Haver, Fred's second wife, wouldn't be there because she had entered a convent in 1953 and didn't meet Fred until her return to Hollywood. My parents stood up for them when they married.

Johnny Weissmuller might let out a Tarzan yell or jump into the pool. The women loved him, and he returned the favor.

Red Skelton would be clowning around at the same time he worried about his television contract. *Everybody* in Hollywood was worrying about the effect of television on the film industry. Dad and Red got into some heavy negotiations with the networks on the rapidly growing new medium.

Dad with Ozzie Olson, greeting Ann Miller,
one of Dad's favorite people

There would even be a few ghosts of those who had meant so much to us and had passed on—Lupe Velez, Carol Landis, and Robert Walker among them.

My grandparents would probably be talking about the fact that they had given my parents' marriage six months at best, and here they were about to celebrate their 30th wedding anniversary. Mother was probably surprised as well, but she loved being surrounded by stars and was proud of Dad's accomplishments.

The men were eyeing all the glamorous women in the room, and the women were looking for friends or lovers or husbands, or perhaps a part in the next movie on the horizon. A few were discreetly exploring same-sex relationships. One of our director clients was present with his current boyfriend. And one writer brought a call girl as his date, and they were discussing marriage.

If Marlene Dietrich was there, she'd be posing, as only she could, those famous cheekbones poised for a photo. Joan Crawford's hungry eyes would take in everything in the room and everybody in it. We'd get an effusive thank-you note in tomorrow's mail, for sure. (Joan was notorious in Hollywood for sending thank-you notes; if you sent her a thank-you note, you'd get a thank-you for your thank-you in return.) Merle Oberon may have been in from Acapulco still complaining about the Cabana Club and trolling for potential guests to entertain in her mansion in Mexico.

Among the women were not only stars but also wives and girlfriends. X was getting ready to divorce Y, putting an end to one of the noisiest relationships in the history of fan magazines. S's girlfriend was standing in the wings, waiting to take over for wife No. 1. L was currently dating M but, being a nymphomaniac, she was always looking around. In fact, at our last party she would

John Wayne, Peter Lawford, Henry Wilcoxen, Red Skelton, and Ben Harold.

17

*Ted and I harmonizing with our Barbershop
Quartet in the Bob and Bo's Saloon set.*

corner a good-looking prospect and raise her arms over her head while her boobs popped out. No kidding!

Gloria Swanson was right in *Sunset Boulevard* when she said, "We *had* faces then." Not every face would be recognizable from the silver screen and Broadway, vaudeville and television. But you'd know their work from their show business credits. Contacts were being made, ideas were bandied about, deals were in the works, and relationships were being formed.

The thread that tied all these people together was business, plain and simple. The motion picture industry in particular and entertainment in general was a business like any other. If we were in Iowa, the subject would be the corn crop, in Detroit it would have been cars, in Chicago meatpacking. Our guests were focused on upcoming pictures, box office receipts, contracts, Academy Awards, Emmy nominations and taxes. Somebody was always scribbling on a napkin or a tablecloth with ideas for making money, putting together film packages, casting, or the bottom line of one project or another. One of the subjects would for certain have been Twentieth Century Fox's decision to film all its movies in Cinemascope with stereophonic sound and the fact that color was coming to television and the effect it might have on costs, box office, and viewers.

And the gossip columnists and society editors were taking notes to put in their columns the next day, which would include covering my charismatic father's position as one of Hollywood's very first and most prominent business managers. For years he worked with major Hollywood stars, handling their finances, crafting their budgets, bailing them out of trouble, and working on their behalf in business negotiations. For many of them he was a close and dear friend who many considered their "Uncle Bö."

Why was I there? I'm his daughter, Carolyn. I put the party together, paid the $50,000 bill, and worked with all these clients as part of his firm.

This is his story as I lived it with him.

Dad on the phone, as usual, at his desk in the Beverly Management Corporation offices. The "panda" was an office mascot.

CHAPTER 2

BACK TO BUSINESS -
TYPICAL OFFICE DAY

The next workday after the party was a Monday, and we were back in the office at Beverly Management Corporation (BMC). Columnist Sheilah Graham described our work as "to save and invest the money earned by glamorous clients, so that when the public has had enough of their pretty faces they will not have to sell their homes and jewels and subsequently make that dramatic but sad trek to the poorhouse." Sam Goldwyn said it more succinctly: "Actors think with their hearts. That's why so many of them die broke."

My father founded Beverly Management Corporation in 1932 to handle the finances of actors, writers, producers, and directors in the motion picture industry. His was one of the very first, if not the first, business management firms of its kind, focusing on the motion picture business. When Dad started his business, "business managers" were basically accountants and bookkeepers, not financial advisers. Dad and others raised the profession to a much higher level of giving investment advice, managing resources, planning cash flow, and so on.

Brandy Brent in her column "Carrousel" wrote that there were "three most prominent business managers in Hollywood— Bö Roos, Morgan Maree and Myrt Blum ... among them they

*Peter Lawford making Dad laugh by pleading
for a raise in his weekly allowance.*

controlled some ten to fifty million dollars in capital funds." (Ten to fifty million dollars was an impressive sum in those days.) In 1951, Irv Kupcinet writing in the *Chicago Sun-Times* added two more names to the list—Charles Goldring and George Temple. My dad remained one of the leading business managers in the movie colony ...and to further quote Kupcinet " a member of that very select group ... the biggest and best known names in ... this group ... between them, they got a corner on the wealth of Hollywood." According to the *Saturday Evening Post* in 1951, "At one point, the combined salaries of Roos's 50-odd clients added up to a quarter of a million dollars every Saturday night."

Today, an actor or actress can earn millions of dollars from a single picture. According to the Internet, Brad Pitt's asking price can be anywhere from $10 million to $30 million a picture. Julia Roberts was the first actress to demand (and get) $20 million for a picture, making her the first woman to break through Hollywood's glass ceiling.

Of course, all our clients wanted fame and fortune. Some never got either. Others were famous and rich for a while until their appeal fizzled. Those who got fame didn't necessarily get fortune, or if they got it, they didn't know how to hang on to it. The problem stemmed in part from the business itself. "Cooking the books" was a common practice in the film business. David O. Selznick said, "The whole industry ... is built on phony accounting" so someone had to keep a sharp eye on the bookkeeping.

The biggest problem was with the "stars," and by that I mean the top actors, producers, directors, and writers, most of whom had no experience with handling money that came in quickly when they were a hit. As silent film star Colleen Moore, who created the flapper, described it, "Most of us had more money than sense." Stars felt they were entitled to spend their income—luxuriously and freely. In one of his films, Cary Grant says, "Money talks ... All it ever said to me was 'goodbye.'" That defined the spending habits of many people in the film business.

*This photo accompanied a magazine story that read:...
"Marguerite Chapman discusses with Roos the possibility of
his taking over her business affairs. Roos doesn't solicit clients;
he has headaches enough with those he already has."*

*Chuck Van Sickle and I in BMC office talking
with Bill Lundigan and his niece.*

My father wanted all his clients to have an income of around $25,000 a year when they were no longer at the top. I don't know when he established the annual target of $25,000. According to the U.S. Bureau of Labor Statistics, the average annual wage of workers was only $1,047 in 1935 and only $3,033 by 1950. Stars with incomes of $25,000 a year during that period would have been able to live very comfortably compared with the general population, but it was not enough to allow them the luxuries they enjoyed when others were footing the bills.

To reach the goal of $25,000, Dad gave his clients a strict allowance, monitored their expenses, and advised them on how to invest, guaranteeing that they didn't have to become extras or carhops or busboys when they became box office poison. Hortense Morton of the *San Francisco Examiner* described it this way: "A star's soul may belong to the Studio, but [BMC] has dibs on the bank balance." Dad's clients were his "kids," and he worked hard

Dad advising Ann Dvorak about his vitamins.

to keep them solvent. If a client wouldn't play by Dad's rules, he was no longer a client.

That Monday after the party was a typical day at the office; nothing went right. I needed a lot of patience to deal with it all.

The worst distraction was the Arthur Andersen taxmen who were using the conference room upstairs to work on several clients' last-minute tax returns and were continually coming down to my office with requests for various documents they needed. (In those days, Arthur Andersen was the top accounting firm in the country.)

In addition, Dad was in the San Fernando Valley at the jungle set for Johnny Weissmuller's new Tarzan movie and called to tell me I had to cover for him with a new client, Peter Lawford, who had an appointment with him within the hour. Peter had been recommended by several other people in the business and was

A brief moment in a day's work in the office...
Dad with Ted and I and a few favorite employees.

coming in to see how we could protect his income from taxes. He was counting on Dad's reputation as "Uncle Deductible."

Added to that was another visit from actor John Carroll, who was quite a lover boy, tall, dark, handsome, charming, and with a terrific voice. Unfortunately, Carroll turned out to be more trouble than he was worth. Dad never had a written contract with a client. They were free to come and go. We let them, but it was disruptive. Carroll would come in periodically, upset about something, pick up his books, and leave. Then he'd be back in a week, turning on the charm and wanting to be a client again. One of these days, I thought, we will just have to harden ourselves and lock the door when he tries to get back in.

It got very complicated for me, handling temperamental and attention-demanding stars, writers, and directors, my charismatic father, the IRS, the gossip columnists, and all the rest.

So how did I get involved in the crazy business?

When I was very little, Dad took me with him to show some prospective buyers a house he had just built, and afterwards he told me that one day I would be his private secretary. I always thought that sounded great, and in high school I concentrated on all the business courses they offered and did quite well in them. My last semester in school, I started working in his office two hours each week for extra credits toward a certificate of recommendation for employment, one of only seven for the graduating class.

After graduation, I gave college a whack and enrolled at the University of Southern California, but backed out at the last minute. After taking a good look around at the social scene and my academic choices, I decided college was not for me. I'd already been to the best parties in Hollywood and Beverly Hills with kids my own age and adults, and had a few boyfriends and a closet full of evening gowns. Some of the guests at my graduation party from *elementary* school had been important Hollywood names such as Betty Grable, Ward Bond, Jackie Coogan, Lupe Velez, and Johnny Weissmuller. It seemed as if college would be like high school all over again. In addition, we were in World War II, which was coloring our choices and affected our priorities in terms of getting on with our lives.

On top of that, I had known for a long time that I wanted to work in my dad's office and have a business career, but at USC, at that time, I couldn't take any business courses until my sophomore year. So, on the one hand I could sit around being a freshman, studying courses I wasn't interested in, or on the other I could go to work for my dad and go to dinner at Chasen's with the likes of Peter Lawford and John Wayne. It wasn't a hard choice. Instead of college, I opted for six months at Sawyers Business School in Westwood, polishing my accounting and shorthand skills.

Finally, I reached my first goal and became a full-time employee for Beverly Management Corporation. Being the boss's daughter entitled me to a start—right at the bottom of the ladder. Cobina Wright may have written in her column that she spotted "The Bö Roos's with their daughter Carolyn and Johnny Weissmuller and his new wife at Penny Singleton's Biltmore Bowl opening," but my working day was a little less glamorous.

Initially, my big domain at the office was the reception area and the telephone switchboard. Even if I say so myself, I not only did the job well, but became well known to clients and other offices in the business. They were flattered when I recognized their voices. I worked hard to make the caller or the person I was calling feel that they were extremely important. I loved being the first person the clients saw as they entered the office. So many experiences were such fun because of the many different celebrities and interesting people around us. Quite a heady experience for an eighteen-year-old! One of our favorite stars, Van Johnson, would stop by and ask me to call back to our accounting department for his checks and bills to be brought to my office, and we would sit and chat. He was so boyish and cute, with his shy smile and his red socks. He and his friends (later our clients also) Keenan Wynn and Robert Walker would flirt and kid with me, as would many of our other male clients. I always laughed and teased back with them. Howard Keel would sing to us; it was like having an MGM musical right in the office. He sure was handsome! Rory Calhoun kept trying to get me to go camping with him and share his bedroll. Red Skelton would get everybody laughing with his clowning. He would come in the office to chat and do crazy things like pretending to stand on his ear. When he did that, pens and pencils dropped out of his pockets, and his rubber face would express dismay. He was always on stage.

I was thrilled when my father started using me as a junior secretary and what was sometimes called a "leg man." A "gopher" was probably a better description, since I was often sent out to the studios or to clients' homes with bills for them to approve and checks or contracts to sign. Every bill had to be okayed by my dad and the client, and they both had to co-sign checks.

Those trips were not as interesting as they might sound. At Joan Crawford's you had to take your shoes off to keep the white carpets in pristine condition. Once we had some documents

Our client, Rex Allen, the singing cowboy and his horse Koko paused
for lunch at the famous corner of Wilshire Blvd. and Rodeo Drive
in the heart of Beverly Hills on their way to the BMC office.

for Marlene Dietrich to sign. Dad's brother, Art, who ran the accounting department, usually got the job, but this time he pleaded not to go. The last time he had called on Dietrich, she had greeted him in a negligee that was as sexy as it was revealing. Art was sort of a stuffed shirt and was upset by the whole thing. I think he may have thought she was trying to seduce him. She may have been! It could have been worse. Actually, a few movie stars would answer the door in the nude, but I don't remember them being our clients.

Sometimes my dad and I would go to the studios together. Usually I'd be taking shorthand in the backseat of our limo, and

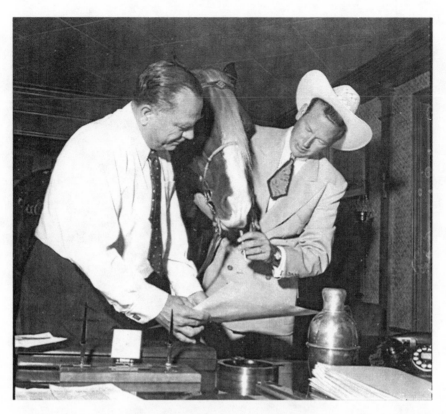

*Rex and Koko in Dad's office watching Rex sign
an up and coming singing contract.*

Dad would be talking on his mobile phone. (He had one of the first mobile phones in Los Angeles, and he said he once got the Kremlin on the phone, whether on purpose or by mistake no one remembers.) At times seeing a major motion picture being filmed was interesting, but more often it was just boring. So much time was spent waiting around while actors were being made up or dressed, learning their lines, or being coached. More time was taken while scenes were being set up, lighting was adjusted, and cameras were moved. The takes took only a few minutes, but some directors insisted on endless retakes. So much time seemed wasted. Often people were surprised that I didn't want to be in movies myself. I knew the stars were treated like a piece of property

Rex taking the time to serenade a few of the staff in the BMC office.

on and off the set. On the set there was always crude language, and there were smart cracks and huge egos from drama kings and queens, which included just about everybody on the set when it came to their special niche. If you wanted to see drama on a really big scale, you had only to study the moguls, among them Louis B. Mayer (MGM), Jack Warner (Warner Brothers), Harry Cohn (Columbia), and Herbert Yates (Republic), who always acted as if they were running kingdoms, not movie studios. I always thought what went on behind the camera was more interesting than what went on in front of it, but I was always glad to get back to the office.

We knew firsthand that acting in particular and the entertainment industry in general was a very unstable business. Actors who were starting in the business were often broke while trying hard to be discovered. Those who were under contract to the studios were often underpaid. In his memoir, *Only Make Believe*, our client Howard Keel said he made only $4,250 for his starring role in the smash hit musical *Seven Brides for Seven Brothers*. In 1958 Howard was president of the Screen Actors Guild and pointed out how important it was that they "laid the groundwork for what is now our Pension and Health Fund ... that's now the best in the world."

Even the top stars were only as good as their last picture and anxiously awaited the next script that would be a box office success and boost their negotiating power. So many actors, writers, producers, and directors who had been in the business a long time were starving, victims of age, changing audience tastes, the economy, and competition from new media.

When I turned nineteen, I had been working for a year at BMC, busy learning how the accounting department worked, learning about insurance requirements, and spending some time in the filing department. My dad's private secretary, Mary Lou May, took me under her wing. She was terrific, and I learned fast. She eventually married the actor Ward Bond, and I wound up taking over her job.

Keeping track of clients was hard enough, but keeping track of my father was not an easy task either. *Daily Variety* described his modus operandi thus: "He made about 60 phone calls a day, commuted by plane around the world, worked with his clients, played poker with them, went to Mexico with them and was said even to weep with them." I have a clipping from the *Herald Examiner* from 1940 that reads: "Talk about service. Bö Roos' actors agency in Hollywood calls Joan Woodbury every day at 8 a.m. to remind her to get up and feed the baby." I don't remember that, but it's a good story.

I had always been "Daddy's Girl" and felt very comfortable working with him. I was proud of his accomplishments. His good looks and his all-enveloping personality could convince anyone that he could do anything. I often told him that he could make people believe that black was white and that apples were blue.

He was a whiz in meetings when he was making contract deals with the studios and the agents for his stars. He always got what he wanted for them, which still amazes me. I loved to sit in on his many meetings to watch him at work. Clients sometimes felt as if he were a magician with special powers, and would tell him so after a particularly difficult contract had been worked out in their favor.

My brother Bö Jr., agrees, saying, "In his prime, this man had no peers. His business was sales, and he could sell any idea he needed to and many he did not need. He operated with so many new techniques in negotiation. When television came along, he was a true pioneer. His connections were worldwide, and even today's tax laws are a mirror of his innovations." Dad was a tiger when it came to finding every possible item that could be deductible and ensuring that it would be deductible. The record keeping drove some clients crazy.

Dad was not above faking things if he had to. My brother remembers receiving a call from Dad in New York one day when Red Skelton would not go on to do his television show. "Dad said, 'Dynie [my brother's nickname], get down on your knees by the bed and cry while you tell him of my heart attack [a lie] and tell him he has to go on—if not for him, for me.' I did so, and Skelton got up and did the show."

As far as working with Dad was concerned, I knew *never* to walk into his office without my steno pad to make notes. He always had several things going at the same time, and it was challenging and exciting to keep up with him. He could be a perfectionist and expected people to meet his high standards. Thankfully, he never got mad at me. He kept the staff on its toes, and most of them wanted to please him.

A typical day at the office for me went something like this:

Field calls from clients, talent agents, publicists, the press, business associates, investors, and so on, usually with problems. Dad was on a very personal basis with each and every client. We got calls from them demanding more money. Wives and ex-wives with problems about their allowances and alimony. Girlfriends upset about something. Talent agents wanting to discuss how to maximize their client's returns on an upcoming contract. Clients in trouble for one reason or another—romantic, marital, parental, business, creative, sometimes alcohol or drug related. Often they'd just pop into the office, without an appointment.

Press agents and columnists were continually trolling for stories, gossip, and insider information. Sometimes we needed to keep clients' names out of the press, rather than in. Most of these were referred to our publicity agent. According to Samantha Barbas in her book, *The First Lady of Hollywood*, a biography of gossip columnist Louella Parsons, there were almost 400 journalists covering Hollywood news in the mid-1930s. The Hollywood press corps was second only to that of Washington, D.C. (Louella's daughter, Harriet Parsons was one of our clients for many years.)

Several people worked on scheduling Dad's appointments, including his assistants at various times such as Bob Schiller, Charlie Trezona (Dad's nephew), and Chuck Van Sickel. Al Marsella worked with Dad's brother, Art, in handling the accounting and tax department. Al is a CPA and tax consultant who is still doing our tax returns. He handled many of our clients through the years and has been and is a trustee for the Fred and June MacMurray estate.

We had twenty or more employees at one time, and everyone made demands on Dad's time. It fell to Dad's secretary to coordinate all of the appointments and mesh everything together, from travel plans to meetings, and to work in his personal activities. There was a lot of correspondence and record keeping. We were legally responsible to clients, the IRS, and so on for keeping careful records of expenditures and investments.

I worked at BMC for twelve years from 1941 to 1953 and off and on beyond that for special events, parties, and hiring and training secretaries and office staff. I spent two years helping close BMC when Dad passed away.

My brother, Bö Jr., worked at BMC from about 1948 to 1958 as an account executive, advising clients and consulting with them on real estate properties, getting signatures on agreements and checks, and working on investments in clubs, golf courses, and so on. And, of course, he helped out wherever needed, as we all did. His accounts included Rory Calhoun, James Arness, Andrew McLaglen, and Howard Keel.

My brother remembers: "Dad did everything he could to increase my desire for the management business, but I wanted to build houses. Dad backed me in my first project with Beverly Wilshire Construction Company, and I was able to learn on the job. We built housing tracts, and I helped build his home in Brentwood in 1956. Shortly after that I left the office and went out on my own building houses."

To show how accounts and projects often overlapped, our client John Wayne was offered the role of Marshal Matt Dillon in the television series *Gunsmoke*. Duke didn't want to commit to a weekly series, so he suggested his friend James Arness, who also became a client. Andrew McLaglen was another client who directed films such as *McLintock* for Batjac (a Wayne company) and also directed *Gunsmoke*. Most of our clients came in through referral from one to another.

A lot of what we had to do was entertaining clients and contacts from out of town. Hotel reservations? Tickets to a play? Invitations to dinner? A list of the hot spots in town? We were accommodating, of course, and people reciprocated when we needed favors.

If somebody wanted to play golf, my brother was always the one called upon to take them out for a round. He says he was raised on a golf course (the California Country Club and Lakeside Country Club) and played mostly under par, with a handicap of 3 to 4. He still plays, but a hip replacement has affected his game. He played often with Howard Keel, a really avid golfer until Howard's death in 2004. Bill Lundigan was pretty good, too. Rory Calhoun preferred fishing and hunting. The Andrews Sisters just clowned around on the course.

It was *not* a typical day at the office when somebody broke into our safe and stole some files in 1952. Coincidentally, two accountants from our office started their own company, taking half a dozen clients with them.

And between all this there were the deals—the hotels in Acapulco and elsewhere in Mexico, Hawaii, and Culver City; the oil drilling in Egypt and Arabia; fishing fleets in South America; the yacht rental; the apartments, ranches, and other real estate; the studio fights; and lots more.

The atmosphere was pretty chaotic. Ben Hecht once wrote that writers worked in a pell-mell atmosphere. We did, too, with phones ringing, people coming and going—everybody with an agenda, an idea, a demand, or a beef.

How did we do it? I'll try to explain.

Father and Daughter... mutual admiration.

*Business Management at work: Dad's clients signing
documents for a joint venture. Looking on are, left ro right:
lawyers, George Henzie and Frank Belcher,
Edna Skelton, Frank Borzage, Robert Walker, Dad,
Harriet Parsons, Ann Dvorak, Leslie Fenton,
Fred MacMurray, Johnny Weissmuller and Red Skelton.*

CHAPTER 3

MONEY MAKES THE
WORLD GO AROUND –

WHAT A BUSINESS MANAGER DOES
AND HOW HE DOES IT

In 1946 and 1947, anthropologist Hortense Powdermaker spent twelve months in Hollywood studying the natives, using some field techniques similar to those she had used in researching South Sea aborigines. One of her conclusions about the movie business was that "natives who have been exposed to American movies classify them into two types, 'kiss-kiss' and 'bang-bang.'" When I think about it, that could be an accurate description of most movies today!

After analyzing various facets of the business, she wrote in her book, *Hollywood; The Dream Factory*, that the job of the business manager consisted of "working out" a budget for his client and family, with specific amounts to be spent for running the house, for clothes, for personal allowances for husband, wife and children, for payments to dependents, for contributions to causes, and for other expenses ... and pays the bills, makes out the various allowance checks, and saves or invests the remainder. This means that there is very little about the actor's life the latter does not know. If a mistress is being supported or there are large losses at cards or on horses, the manager knows it." According to our CPA Al Marsella, Dad "gave one of his clients a hard time when the client would not admit that he was not reporting his gambling winnings and also some special project money to which BMC would be entitled its 5% management fee. He would look at me and say, 'Give them the books.' It was his way of saying goodbye. Dad never insisted on signed contracts; a handshake would do because, as he said, "then you are a living contract."

What a business manager does has not changed very much over the years. A recent article in the *New York Times* about current business managers was headlined "Making Sure Hollywood's Nouveau Riche Stay Rich" and described their job as "keeping stars from spending themselves blind." "Entourage busting" is what sometimes has to be done, especially with young clients. Evan Bell, one of the managers quoted, reported that he recently had a twenty-one-year-old client with fourteen people living in her house. His advice: "kick everyone out." Another manager, Scott Feinstein, said he received a call from a client in his mid-twenties who wanted to buy a $35,000 watch. Feinstein asked him, "What time does it say?" When the client said, "Ten minutes after 3," Feinstein told him, "Mine says 10 after 3, too, and it cost me 60 bucks. Put the watch down."

In the 1930s and 1940s a star's management team pretty much consisted of an agent, a publicity person, and a business manager. Back then, agents and business managers acted as personal managers as well, getting much more involved in a client's personal life than most managers today, when personal managers are common. In an article in *The New Yorker* by Tad Friend about the head of the William Morris Agency, he wrote, "In the nineteen-thirties, legend had it that agents wouldn't order tomato juice in public, lest someone joke that they were drinking their clients' blood." It was rare for a client not to complain about his or her agents. They seldom realized that their financial problems stemmed from their own overspending or dips in popularity, too many romances, or expensive vices.

Attending industry functions was a part of the job. Frank Borzage and Dad second from left with John Wayne and Jack Carson to the right.

Kay Mulvey and Marion Frey wrote in *Cosmopolitan* magazine that "The Hollywood business manager staves off diamond-mine promoters, passes on prospective husbands, hires and fires servants, answers kidnap notes; he handles touches, charity requests, spoiled parents and blackmail." Powdermaker wrote that a business manager is "accustomed to receiving phone calls at all hours to come to the aid of his clients. One phones at six in the morning that he is in trouble at a gambling joint, and will the business manager come quickly. The trouble may be money or a fight. Or the wife of a client calls him, angry and excited, to tell him that her husband came home drunk at four a.m. and crawled into bed with the maid, and she is never going to sleep with him again and is going to start divorce proceedings at once. The business manager rushes over and effects a reconciliation. The wife remains, but the maid leaves."

*A serious business discussion with Frank Borzage, Antonio
Diaz Lombardo (Bank of Mexico), Lloyd Nolan and
Dad... probably about their investment in Mexico.*

That was the kind of crazy business we were in, and it fit
Dad's personality like a glove. He was a natural, quickly making
a name for himself in the industry. He was a flamboyant, high-
powered, fun-loving person whom Lloyd Shearer in an article in
Liberty magazine described as "a big easy-going St. Bernard of a
man who seems to thrive on the work. He has a calm, reassuring
temperament, and nothing ruffles him, not even tantrum active
actresses."

Dad thought that a star making more than $25,000 a year
needed a star business manager who had the ability, the financial
savvy, and the power and clout in the business to handle the
financial, personal, and social demands of high-powered clients.
He fit the bill to a tee. He was dapper, always well dressed, at ease
with people from all walks of life, and a man about town with
connections all over the world.

Some years were nonstop. Because of Dad's popularity and
the many articles about how he was saving the motion picture

stars so much money, we actually had to turn away prospective clients. Some of them would come in already so much in debt that it would be just too much work to get them out of the hole they had dug for themselves. When that happened, we would recommend some other business manager or good accountant and hope they could get themselves some help.

Of course, a star's income in the "old days" was very different from today. Silent film star Francis X. Bushman was considered a phenomenon for having made 424 films and earned a total of $6 million for five years' work, a huge amount of money at the time. In 1942 the head of MGM, Louis B. Mayer, earned more than anyone in the United States, with an income of $949,765. Bob Hope was making a mere $294,166.67. It was still a lot of money, but it took a lot of doing to hang on to it. By the way, I was earning $90 a week.

Mayer would probably roll over in his grave if he saw what stars are making nowadays. So would my father. According to *Parade* magazine's special report "What People Earn" in the March 13, 2005, issue, the annual incomes of some current stars were as follows:

> Jessica Simpson: $4 million
> Lindsay Lohan at age 18: $10 million
> Catherine Zeta-Jones: $18 million
> Renee Zellwegger: $21 million
> John Travolta: $25 million
> Angelina Jolie $27 million

It's even more amazing what sports figures earn. Lance Armstrong bicycled his way to $19 million. Those are annual earnings, but the value of a single contract nowadays also boggles the mind. Kobe Bryant signed a seven-year, $136.4 million contract with the Lakers. In 2004 quarterback Michael Vick of the Atlanta Falcons became the richest player in the NFL by signing a ten-year, $130 million contract extension that guaranteed him

$37 million in bonuses. Add to that endorsements, speaking engagements, public appearances, book deals, and who knows what else, and the total can skyrocket.

Dad would have loved doing business with them!

The Associated Press's Bob Thomas quoted Dad as saying that when we got a client, we would take three or four months to survey his or her financial structure. The "we" in our office included tax, insurance, real-estate, and legal specialists. Digging out financial information from clients was not always easy, as exemplified by a big film executive who got in a jam and asked Dad to straighten out his tangled affairs. "The first thing we better do," said Dad, "is make up a list of your assets and liabilities." "That," screamed the big shot, "is none of your business!"

As expected, our biggest set of problems stemmed from our clients themselves. Most of the motion picture people were unprepared for the large sums of money they were earning all of a sudden. One writer said that Hollywood was a gold mine where you could make $100,000 a week "for two weeks" and then you never got hired again. Dad would explain to his "kids" that his job was to ensure that they had enough money to live comfortably when they were not working and to help them save toward their future when they were no longer "stars." He had seen too many of them wind up as carhops, busboys, extras, or salesclerks when they became box office poison. Few of the stars were realistic enough to realize that they could wind up broke, as Veronica Lake did. Larry McShane of the Associated Press wrote that she had been the "it-girl of the 1940's silver screen" and died "penniless three decades later" with "offers for her ashes from potential buyers."

The money flowed out quickly. Van Johnson was one of our most popular clients, earning just less than $1,000 a week in 1945, when the average wage earner was making $44.20 a week. Sheilah Graham, writing in the Washington, D.C., *Sunday Star,* explained how the money "vanished"—20 percent withholding tax, 10 percent to the agent, 3½ percent to the business manager,

10 percent for war bonds, one half of 1 percent to the Motion Picture Relief Fund, 5 percent for publicity, and 20 percent for taxes. That all added up to 70 percent of their income, without *any* money spent on living expenses.

We worked valiantly to try to get the client's living expenses down. Often a star would be spending $2,000 a month when he should have been spending $1,000. Stars were not necessarily spendthrifts. Living was automatically higher for them. They always had to look like movie stars. Joan Crawford once said that if you want to see the girl next door, go next door. Meanwhile she had to look like a movie star at all times, even when taking out the garbage (as if she ever did!). Part of the image was a lavish home, chauffeurs, insurance, private school for the kids, beauty treatments, clothes. Add to that voice and diction lessons, maybe an alimony check or two, and the expenses added up quickly. The studios loved to see a star put on a big front, but the business manager knew the perils of overspending. As Morgan Maree, another business manager, once said, "In this town you can be making $400,000 a year and still be penniless."

Once we assessed their financial situation, we established a budget. It was not easy to keep the spending in line. Stars felt they had earned the money, and that it was theirs to spend. Wives, girlfriends, and mistresses especially chafed at the spending restrictions.

Our client Rory Calhoun got his option lifted once and received a hefty salary increase from the studio. He thought that justified a raise from his allowance of $35 a week. Dad didn't agree. It got down to Rory saying, "It's my money, and I want it." Dad's reply was, "Of course you can have it, but please find yourself another business manager." In the end, Rory backed down and left with his $35-a-week allowance intact. He's lucky Dad didn't make him take less! Then we had to keep records of all a client's expenses and income. Some stars were very careless in their record keeping. Others were fussy in reviewing the books and signing their checks. Once after director Frank Borzage had quickly signed $50,000 worth of checks, he stopped cold and demanded an explanation when one popped up for $13 for "miscellaneous expenses."

One of our biggest female stars went into Dad's office with plans to add a larger stable to her ranch home and a cabana by the swimming pool, but by the time Dad had gotten through to her, "she left feeling the hot breath of the poorhouse on her neck." The wife of another client needed new slipcovers for her living room furniture. The old ones were in tatters. Dad's advice? Take the money out of your $50-a-week allowance.

Our next set of problems were the studios. Working with the star's agent, we would set up how our clients got paid and how much in any one year. The studios would have preferred to deal with actors rather than businessmen, but that was our job. We were always looking for ways to make better deals for our clients. Dad was a tough negotiator. Our priority was to make the best possible profit for our stars with the least possible risk financially.

In earlier years, stars worked basically for a salary, but in the late 1940s that changed to a sharing of profits. Our staff discussions often involved how income on a project would be split between talent, directors, producers, studios, and others involved. Should we settle for a guarantee, a percent of the gross, a percent of the profit, or, more likely, a combination thereof? Most studios preferred deals that involved a percent of the profit. After all, they thought, you can't split a profit unless there is one. Unfortunately, profit had a way of disappearing from view when Hollywood's creative approaches to finance were involved. Maybe it would be better to stretch out the payments? I heard that Jane Russell was paid over a period of twenty years for her work in *The Outlaw*. Every situation was different.

Deals were made and remade. If in the middle of a picture a star discovered that someone else had a better deal, he would push his agent and business manager to go into action to remake his contract. Dad and the William Morris Agency were involved with several such situations. In her book, *Mr. & Mrs. Hollywood* about Lew Wasserman, head of MCA, Kathleen Sharp mentions lucrative and innovative contract arrangements for clients such as Red Skelton. Another example was when MCA came up "with the idea of selling Amos and Andy to CBS as a corporation, not as individual actors ... That way the talent wouldn't have to pay 77 percent of its income in taxes, but a lower corporate rate of only 25 percent."

Taxes were always a problem. There was a federal income tax in 1862 to help pay for the Civil War, but the income tax as we know it started in 1913 and has been hounding us ever

Dad "lobbying" Congressman Don Jackson and Los Angeles County Supervisor Leonard Roach for improving benefits for the Stars and creating a favorable climate for the film industry in Southern California through changes in the tax codes and other tax laws. Looking on is longtime friend Art La Shelle.

since. As the movies started "talking" and the stars started making money, the government seemed to come up with more and more ideas to raise money, often as a temporary measure that became permanent. The tax laws keep changing and are so complicated that somebody said it takes more brains to file your taxes than it takes to make the income. With the complex income situations for our clients, we had to pay attorneys and tax consultants to keep us constantly on track.

Dad became known as "Uncle Deductible" or "Mister Deductible." He had an almost missionary zeal to find legitimate deductions for clients. According to Al Marsella, when Dad was interviewed by a magazine as a leading business manager, he claimed, "Everything is deductible with regard to taxes." Al says, "This statement got him into hot water with the IRS when they read the article. The IRS audited Bö and Beverly Management for something like the prior six years or so. We came out of the audit okay, but they asked Bö to do some things that he would not do, one of which was to get affidavits from maitre d's, bellhops, waiters, etc., to back up some of his deductions. We refused because it might get them in trouble with the IRS as they probably never reported the big tips Bö would dish out."

Erskine Johnson, who had a column as well as a radio show on KHJ in Los Angeles, reported that, "Roos told him that he had a perennial beef with the man with the whiskers and the tall hat. The income tax laws he says are definitely unfair for actors. He feels that everybody gets to deduct something for depreciation. Farmers get 33 1/3 percent. Oilmen get 17 percent. He feels that there should be depreciation on an actor's ability. As he said, an actor spends 10 years struggling for recognition, and when they click, the minute they become successful the government takes 90 percent of their salary. The average life of a star's limelight is five years. After five years of paying 90 percent to the government, they are washed up with very little in the bank ... It's enough to make you cry Uncle! or Uncle Sam! Roos feels that something should be done about it."

In addition to lobbying for breaks for people in the film industry, Dad and other business managers created tax shelters for their clients by having them invest in a wide variety of business deals. Unlike other business managers, though, Dad invested right alongside his clients. As he said, "I ride every deal in which I ask my clients to invest their money. If they make money, I do, too. If they lose, I'm right there with them." In 1951 alone, Dad was a partner in sixteen business ventures.

Moneymaking opportunities were always being sent to us. In fact, Dad cultivated a wide array of banks, builders, business executives, and others to keep us alert to legitimate investments. No investment is a sure bet, but we got a slew of offers for "once in a lifetime" get-rich schemes from fans, con men, and connivers that seemed like sure losers. According to columnist Lloyd Shearer writing in *Liberty* magazine, one woman wrote Fred MacMurray, "I know you are just an actor, and like most actors you probably have no business brains. I am therefore going to give you an opportunity to invest $25,000 in a chain of roller skating rinks." Bing Crosby was approached to invest in the manufacture of "breathe-easy brassieres." In 1950 alone, we received forty-eight business offers that involved from $2,000 to $2,500,000 investment. We sent gold mines and oil deals to the legal department. Inventions went to another department. And sick businesses went to an office manager for evaluation.

I think Dad's all-time favorite investment was real estate, a business he knew from the ground up. Once he told Joan Crawford to sell her fancy house and buy an apartment. She listened carefully, then kept the house *and* bought the apartment building (In fact, that apartment building is still standing on the corner of Rodeo Drive and Charleville in Beverly Hills.)

I remember proofreading copy for an article about him that was about to appear in a national magazine. Part of it said: "Beverly Management Corporation managed about five to seven million dollars in a typical year and a great deal of it was invested in real estate, cattle ranches, oil wells and various other tax shelters. Roos showed his clients how they had the ability to gross more than most corporations by careful planning and investment. He has put most of his stars into the real estate field and feels that it is the best advantage for their money."

Initially, BMC charged our clients 3½ percent as a fee for handling their finances; later it went up to 5 percent. We must have done something right to retain many clients for years, but Dad always claimed that he couldn't make any money off the percentage because his overhead was so high, including staff salaries and expert advice. Not all investments were successful. There was always an element of risk, and some involved our biggest clients, such as John Wayne. Details of some of the deals, including the ones that went awry, are in later chapters. I have ledger sheets in my files from some of our clients detailing their ongoing expenses. There was a flood of checks that went out the door of BMC—checks for allowances for the star, household allowances for wives, payments to family members, secretaries, mistresses, gardeners, maids, butlers, publicists, and chauffeurs, insurance payments, tuitions, rents, and utilities. Professional dues had to be paid to the Screen Actors Guild and the American Federation of Radio Artists. Commissions were paid to agents and publicists and BMC. Alimony checks went out regularly, as did payments on loans. I love the ones for minor expenses such as these: Encyclopedia Britannica—7th of the month—$25.20 use coupons; Tom's Rubbish Service—$16 a month; Dorothy Lamour's rental of a typewriter for $8.97 every three weeks; and Joan Crawford's rent on a Singer sewing machine for $5 a month.

Beyond business, business managers had to function as diplomats. In his autobiography, *Walking the Tightrope*, Henry Rogers wrote that Dad's clients represented some 25 percent of Rogers and Cowan's entire public relations business and that Dad consistently recommended his clients to them. When the House Un-American Activities Committee was in full swing, Dad called Henry and told him he was in trouble because "one of my most important clients ... is pressuring me to pull all of our clients out of your office." Dad brokered a meeting for John Wayne and filmmaker Carl Foreman in the BMC offices that led to an hours-long debate between the two men, who were on opposite sides of the political spectrum. It didn't change their minds, but it did lead to a "cease-fire" of sorts as far as business was concerned. By 1952, Henry Rogers said Rogers & Cowan had become the biggest and most successful publicity firm in Hollywood.

Business management is and was never easy, never dull, and always challenging.

Below is one of the many "thank you letters" received from Joan Crawford. This one was received following my dad's death.

JOAN CRAWFORD

October 1, 1973

Billie dear,

Thank you for your very sweet letter and for giving me your new address in Newport Beach. I know that area, and it's lovely and peaceful there - I hope you are enjoying your home, and this period of adjustment is working out well for you, dear friend.

I hope too that I will see you when I am in California again.

Love, as ever,

Joan

*A favorite photo of Mom an Dad, both looking
happy as they started a vacation in Hawaii.*

CHAPTER 4

MOM & DAD

My father, Bö Christian Roos, and my mother, Gladys Landl Holmes, made an unusual couple, and both were responsible for the family's success.

My father was born in Los Angeles in 1903 and named after his father, Bö Christian Roos, who was born in Sweden in 1842. I have a genealogical chart that indicates the family as a "noble dynasty, Roos Af Hyjelmsater, introduced 1625 to the House of Nobles, Stockholm, Sweden."

Grandfather Roos, nicknamed Chris Roos, graduated from Upsala University in Sweden as a mechanical steam–electric engineer. He sailed the Seven Seas and landed in New York Harbor. He had been known to build the first hydro-electric plant in the West. I am not sure what else he did for a living, but several years later, in 1890, he married my grandmother Anna Katherine Butt in San Francisco. Her parents had emigrated from Germany and settled in San Francisco, where they owned a saloon and a market.

Grandfather and Grandmother set up housekeeping in Los Angeles and had three sons, my father being the youngest. My grandfather Chris was known as a rugged Swede and a strict disciplinarian, and he lived by the Golden Rule. He had many friends, was devoted to his family, and loved America. He was sixty-one when my father was born and died when my father was only seven years old.

ROOS of HJELMSÄTER

GRANDFATHER
Bo Christian
1803 to 1841
Sweden

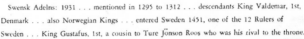

Swensk Adelns: 1931 . . . mentioned in 1295 to 1312 . . . descendants King Valdemar, 1st, Denmark . . . also Norwegian Kings . . . entered Sweden 1451, one of the 12 Rulers of Sweden . . . King Gustafus, 1st, a cousin to Ture Jönson Roos who was his rival to the throne.

FATHER
Bo Christian
1842 Sweden to
1908 Los Angeles

175 ROOS
Swensk—1451

BO, SR'S FATHER . . .

1863 . . . "Chris" Roos graduated Upsala University, Sweden, Mechanical Steam-Electric Engineer . . . He sailed the seven seas, landing in New York Harbor in 1867 . . . Worked for John Ericsson (Inventor and builder of the famous USS Monitor) . . . 1869, organized a Banker, Broker and Travel Agent business, Branches in Göteborg and Liverpool . . . raised to Master Mason, Nassau Lodge #536 . . . received Royal Arch Degree, Grand Chapter #148 in 1874, New York City . . . 1885 . . . Mechanical Supt. Anaconda Smelters, Butte & Helena, Montana . . . 1889 . . . Supt. Edison Gas & Electric Co., San Rafael, Calif. . . . 1890 married Anna Katherine Butt, who was born 1864 in San Francisco . . . 1893 . . . Supt. J. R. Lloyd Electric Co., San Bernardino, Calif. building first Hydro-Electric plant in the West, on Mill Creek . . . 1897 . . . came to Los Angeles, opened a Gas, Electric Fixture and Supply business at 115 North Main Street (now a part of the New City Hall park) . . .

"Chris" was a rugged Swede, a strict disciplinarian. He lived by the Golden Rule; he loved life and people, which accounted for his many friends . . . he was generous to a fault . . . he was devoted to his family and loved America.

HERE HE IS
Bo Christian
1903 Los Angeles

HIS SON
Bo Christian
1927 Los Angeles

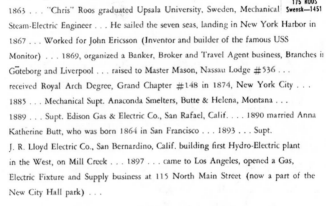

PETER NICOLAUS BUTT
(1829—Hanover, Germany)
Who sailed around the Horn many years are Bo, Sr., was born . . . His Grandfather . . . 1849

1st GENERATION

UNCLE NICK   AUNT DORA   HIS MOTHER   UNCLE GUS

HIS MOTHER

HIS FATHER

2nd GENERATION

ART   BO   ED

*A page from a Tribute book put together by my Uncle
Ed Roos, tracing the Roos Family history.*

The family was not well-to-do, and my grandmother worked for the City of Los Angeles writing records, since she had beautiful handwriting. My father's older brothers helped with the finances. The eldest brother, Bö Christian Edward Roos (who was ten years older than my dad), was in the navy, and the middle one, Arthur Carl Herman Roos (who was eight years older than my father), was an accountant.

Of course, I never knew my grandfather Roos at all, and I don't remember too much about my grandmother Roos since she died when I was about ten years old. I do remember that she had three fig trees in the back yard, which we climbed to get to the figs. She loved watching for the Helms bakery man who delivered baked goods every day to the neighborhood. There was a swing on her front porch that we loved to play on when we visited.

My father had to scramble for money, and he often told us about how he shared a paper route with his best friend, Art La Shelle, when they were seven or eight years old. They had to go past a cemetery during their rounds and were spooked every time and "ran like hell." The two remained friends throughout their lives.

My mother's family had emigrated from England and Scotland, and my granddad was born in Social Circle, Georgia, where his father had owned a plantation. My grandad Holmes left home when he was sixteen and worked on farms and at odd jobs, learned to be a barber, and wound up in St. Louis, Missouri, where he met my grandmother in 1899 when she was working as a cashier in Forest Park Highlands Amusement Park. They were married on January 2, 1900, and went back to Georgia, where my mother was born on June 12, 1903. They named her Gladys Landl Holmes, but she was soon called Billie, a nickname she carried the rest of her life.

Granddad Holmes was one of those people who was ambitious and not afraid to tackle new things. He really proved to be an inspiration to the whole family, including Dad. When people talk of "career paths" nowadays, I think back to all the various careers our family has pursued, especially in real estate, and I

Grandmother and Grandfather Holmes

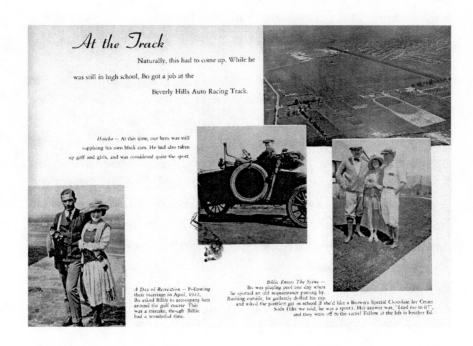

At the Track

Naturally, this had to come up. While he was still in high school, Bo got a job at the Beverly Hills Auto Racing Track.

Hotcha — At this time, our hero was still supplying his own black cars. He had also taken up golf and girls, and was considered quite the sport.

A Day of Recreation — Following their marriage in April, 1922, Bo asked Billie to accompany him around the golf course. This was a mistake, though Billie had a wonderful time.

Billie Enters The Scene — Bo was playing pool one day when he spotted an old acquaintance passing by. Rushing outside, he gallantly doffed his cap and asked the prettiest gal in school if she'd like a Brown's Special Chocolate Ice Cream Soda (like we said, he was a sport). Her answer was, "Lead me to it!", and they were off to the races! Fellow at the left is brother Ed.

Mom and Dad during their "courting days".

credit Granddad Holmes with paving the way, being a teacher and mentor, and setting an example. Grandmother went right along with his ambitions, and throughout their lives they made a hardworking team.

After their marriage, Granddad Holmes suspected that he had tuberculosis, the same disease that killed his father, so they moved to a dry climate, which was supposed to cure TB. They first went to Austin, Texas, then El Paso, and finally to the border town of Douglas, Arizona, which was right across the street from Agua Prieta, Mexico. Granddad Holmes had a barbershop, then a restaurant next door that he and Grandmother owned and operated. Their home was an adobe one that he had built, with a cow and chickens in the back yard. He got an offer from someone to buy the place, so he sold it, bought a lot up the street, and built a brick house. That one sold, too, and before he knew it, Granddad was in the building business. Grandmother was in charge of painting and decorating.

After building houses in Tulsa, Oklahoma, Long Beach, California, and Fort Worth, Texas, the family finally settled in Los Angeles. My mother remembered that she went to six different high schools. Mother was a real "Georgia peach," pretty and popular. She was known as the "sweetheart" of the football team at one of her high schools.

She and my father met at a soda shop near Los Angeles High School and were together almost every evening for the next year until her parents consented to their getting married. My grandparents worried about Dad's having dropped out of high school and the fact that my parents were so young. .

Mother described their wedding: "We were married in Santa Barbara, California, on April 2, 1923, at the home of a Christian Church minister. My mother and father and Bö's mother went with us. We found a park nearby, and we had a picnic lunch. Mother had brought her fried chicken, biscuits, potato salad, and dessert. Dad had loaned us his Ford coupe for our honeymoon because Bö's car was a wreck."

I have been told that they were against the marriage and were known to have said that they gave the marriage six months at most. I also heard, through the years, that my father's brother Ed had made arrangements through a General he knew to have my father accepted to Annapolis. Since my father had left high school before graduation and got married, those plans were derailed. Years later, Los Angeles High School sent Dad an honorary diploma.

Mother's parents gave them a new double bungalow all furnished and ready to live in for their wedding present. Mother wrote, "We rented the other side of the double, and with that money and what little your father earned at his insurance job, we managed. I had saved the money earned working in the bank in the summertime to pay for my first baby. A good thing because Carolyn arrived in December! My father gave me a monthly allowance which helped a lot! My father also bought me a Maxwell sedan car."

Granddad Holmes also got Dad started in business, not only giving him a helping hand but teaching him the lessons he would put to good use over the years. As Mom described it, "About this time Dad decided he would have to do something more to help us! He decided to teach Bö how to build houses. Bö worked as a laborer at first so he learned the right way, from the ground up. That is how he learned all about real estate and finally used the three forms of knowledge (insurance, building and real estate) and was able to form a company." Dad had also studied accounting. Mom went on to write, "Bö seemed to have a knack of being able to manage people. So after he met Ben Lyon and Bebe Daniels he really got into the management business in a big way and opened up The Beverly Management Corporation. He also formed the Insurance Service Bureau and the Beverly Wilshire Construction Company. Through the following years we built and lived in six double bungalows and six single homes, two apartment buildings, and one duplex."

Los Angeles and Beverly Hills had become fertile grounds for a builder in the early 1900s. In 1910 there were few homes in Beverly Hills, but by the '20s the population had increased by 2,500 percent. My granddad eventually built 150 homes in Southern California, and my father also built many homes in Beverly Hills. They concentrated on homes , small bungalows, and duplexes at first,and then big apartment buildings later on. When I graduated from elementary school, we moved into a large apartment complex that the two of them built jointly. It was right across the street from Beverly Hills High School, and I remember Fred MacMurray was a part owner.

My mother's parents and Mom and Dad built adjoining homes and lived next door to each other for more than twenty years.

They say opposites attract, and my parents were certainly opposites in many ways. They were both good-looking. Dad was big, hearty, flamboyant. She was petite, delicate. He was a go-getter, very outgoing, brash, short tempered, emotional. She was reserved, dignified, somewhat cool. He was fiercely independent and had to fend for himself financially from an early age. She was a Southern belle, very close to her parents. He brought his drive to the marriage and was ambitious, well liked, smart, popular. She had social status, was pretty, and had a successful and supportive father. Since Dad had lost his own father at an early age, maybe Granddad Holmes was a substitute for him in a way.

Granddad was a real patriarch. My brother, Bö, says, "W. W. was my dearest, closest friend in the family. He created a place for everybody. Backed everybody. He organized everything for the family."

I've often wondered what my parents got from each other. Mom didn't get the faithful, sober, stay-at-home husband she had hoped for. She did get a lot more excitement than she would probably otherwise have had, plus the chance to travel and meet important, interesting people and entertain many of them in her home. As a young teenager, my mother had been an avid collector of movie star pictures and had several scrapbooks containing movie

Mom and Dad attend the Royal Tiki Ball. Mom was Chairman. Also Mom took time out to join in a picture with June Haver and Marion Nixon. June was married to actor Fred MacMurray and Marion was married to actor and director Ben Lyon.

stars. She was star struck and remained that way throughout her marriage. Dad had a star quality about him, and maybe he dazzled her with his oversize personality and his circle of star clients and friends.

For his part, Dad got a classy, attractive lady for a wife. She was a terrific hostess who could present a good front to his important contacts. She was a great homemaker; our house always ran smoothly even with Dad's erratic schedule. She was a good mother, though not terribly demonstrative in her affections. (Part of that may have been a sign of the times. In those days, people didn't "let it all hang out.") My brother calls Mom "the foundation of the marriage, the one who kept it together. She was upbeat, pleasant, patient ... a marvelous hostess, and a leader."

Someone wrote, "the wife of an extraordinary man must be as extraordinary to keep company with the chiefs of major corporations and heads of State," and Mom had impeccable taste and manners. She was certainly a social leader. I have a lovely picture of her when she was chairman of the Royal Tiki Ball celebrating the twentieth anniversary of the prestigious Bel-Air Guild of Children's Hospital. Rudy Vallee was master of ceremonies and performed at the event.

Their conflicts came from the fact that Dad was not a stay-at-home type. Sitting by the fire toasting marshmallows while the world buzzed around him was simply not his style. Dad joined many of the Hollywood gang by having extramarital affairs, which was made especially easy with his heavy travel plans. Affairs were commonplace in the business. The *Los Angeles Times* obituary for Mildred Shay, a 1930s Hollywood actress, described her social life as "brimming with tales of thwarted casting-couch seductions and affairs with famous men ... She fought off the advances of actors Errol Flynn and Johnny Weissmuller," and she said every time she turned around, "there was someone propositioning me," including Louis B. Mayer and producer Lewis J. Selznick. Her affair with Victor Mature made headlines. I think many of the stars and starlets would have been insulted if a man *didn't* make a pass at them. That was a long time before anybody had heard of "sexual harassment."

Extramarital affairs weren't confined to Hollywood. In many circles it was an accepted part of being a powerful man. I think of Rose Kennedy and Jackie and other women of the Kennedy clan whose husbands were world-class womanizers. The wives knew what was going on but nevertheless stayed in the marriages. Obviously the benefits outweighed the drawbacks.

In Hollywood when you look back at all the movie stars and all their affairs and marriages, you can see that was true. Hollywood infidelities kept the divorce courts and the fan magazines in business. Nicky Hilton, one of many of Liz Taylor's husbands, boasted that one of his conquests would "go down in my little black book along with another three or four hundred stars and starlets." One of Nicky's conquests was John Wayne's second wife, Chata, a story covered later in this book.

Evelyn Keyes in her memoir, *I'll Think About That Tomorrow*, wrote, "that men making sexual overtures to females was considered quite acceptable ... par for the course." But the men "wouldn't give you the job if they thought you slept around. That they didn't approve of, at all. It was a kind of lingering turn-of-the-century good girl versus bad girl mentality."

Columnist Sheilah Graham, who was F. Scott Fitzgerald's mistress, wrote in her book *A State of Heat* that "Wives should watch out when a man is reaching fifty. Men like to preen themselves like the peacock ... They must have a new young mirror to reflect the virility that will soon pass into old age. The clever wife looks the other way ... Women who jump hastily into divorce can find themselves alone when they are too old to hunt for, or want, another husband or companion ... The wise wife hangs on until the storm passes. Usually her husband is glad that she did. It is cheaper to stay married to the first woman, and when you are old you share a solid wedge of the past."

It was many years later that I even discussed this situation with my mother. I had learned that when my younger brother was just six months old, my father had left with the wife of a well-known bandleader . They evidently changed their minds and returned before any damage was done. Each wound up having long marriages with their original spouses. My father and his good friend from high school days, Art La Shelle, traded girlfriends all their lives.

I broke up more than one of my father's affairs. He wasn't above misrepresenting his marital status, Once there was even an ex-girlfriend of John F. Kennedy, courtesy of Sinatra's Rat Pack. She was a lovely woman with two cute kids, and I didn't want to see her hurt.

In those days a line was drawn between a wife and a mistress or girlfriend. Mike Oliver wrote in his column, "Mike Oliver's Acapulco", that once at the Hotel Los Flamingos, attorney Frank Belcher's mistress "had been wearing a bikini and a beach boy, simultaneously. She sat with Bö and his wife Billie, and allowed the beach boy to paw her all over until Roos put his foot down ... he said, 'I won't have this at my table, especially in front of my wife.'" The incident led to an eventual parting of the ways for Dad and his attorney.

I suppose, looking back, that my life with my father was not only not ordinary, but probably unhealthy for me. His name was linked with many female stars, but growing up I thought it was mostly business, whether it was stepping out to nightclubs or getting calls in the middle of the night. I found myself involved to the point that I was privy to his "other life." I must have romanticized what was going on. When I was pregnant with my first child, I think it finally sank in. It really bothered me to have been so naive.

My parents would squabble often, most of the time about trivial things. Maybe it was Mom's way of asserting herself.

My son Denis remembers Dad always yelling, "BILL--EEEE!!!," and that she would just ignore him and go about her business. The two of them had a special whistle they used to summon each other. She could do a whistle as loud as a truck driver. She had us laughing many, many times over that.

If Dad was guilty of something, he would send flowers to Mom and say he worshipped the ground she walked on. The size of the bouquet was bigger if he had had a bit too much to drink. Mom did not drink except on very rare occasions; he did and generally could hold his liquor.

Nevertheless, no matter how much my father complained and how much my mother suffered, they still came back together. They each had countless opportunities to split. And Mother would have had full support from her parents. On their fiftieth wedding anniversary, they celebrated by having a ceremony with their children and grandchildren standing up with them and all their friends around. My mother finally got a nice celebration of her wedding.

I think we all knew their feelings for each other were strained by that time, but there was also a deep love under it all. For years, I had felt like a mouse mediating between two cats. Maybe it wasn't a fairy tale romance, but as Clare Booth Luce wrote in her play *The Women*, "It is being together at the end that counts." Fifty years later Mom and Dad were still together. It took his death to part them.

My parents' renewal of vows and 50th wedding anniversary celebration. Standing up for them were left to right, Two of Bö Jr.'s daughters, Marta and Heidi, my daughter Cathy, me, Mom, Dad, my brother Bö and my sons Denis and Jon Olsen.

My son Jon soloing with the famous violinist Murray Korda.
Mr. Korda was one of my father's favorite musicians.

NOVEMBER 5 1946

SALVADOR DUHART M INSPECTOR
GENERAL OF CONSULATES OF
MEXICAN GOVERNMENT
WASHINGTON D C

IT IS MY DESIRE TO ATTEND INAUGURATION HOWEVER MY WIFE WILL BE

UNABLE TO ACCOMPANY ME   I WILL WIRE ANTONIO DIAZ LOMBARDO

TO MAKE DEFINITE ARRANGEMENTS REGARDING RESERVATIONS BEST REGARDS

BO C ROOS

Chg Beverly Management Corp
400 No Camden Drive
Beverly Hills, Calif.

THE COMPANY WILL APPRECIATE SUGGESTIONS FROM ITS PATRONS CONCERNING ITS SERVICE

WESTERN UNION (59).

SYMBOLS
DL=Day Letter
NL=Night Letter
LC=Deferred Cable
NLT=Cable Night Letter
Ship Radiogram

A. N. WILLIAMS, CHAIRMAN OF THE BOARD   JOSEPH L. EGAN, PRESIDENT

The filing time shown in the date line on telegrams and day letters is STANDARD TIME at point of origin. Time of receipt is STANDARD TIME at point of destination

SA201 47=ZV WASHINGTON DC 4 253P   1946 NOV 4 PM 1 22

B C ROOS=

BEVERLY MANAGEMENT 400 CAMDEN DR LOSA=

WITH REFERENCE INVITATION YOU RECEIVED TO ATTEND INAUGURATION
PRESIDENT ALEMAN MEXICO CITY DECEMBER FIRST KINDLY WIRE ME
MEXICAN EMBASSY NOT LATER THAN NOVEMBER SEVENTH WHETHER YOU
ARE ATTENDING AND WHETHER YOU WILL BE ACCOMPANIED BY YOUR WIFE.
INFORMATION REQUIRED URGENTLY TO MAKE HOTEL RESERVATION IN
MEXICO CITY=

SALVADOR DUHART M INSPECTOR GENERAL OF CONSULATES OF
MEXICAN GOVERNMENT.

THE COMPANY WILL APPRECIATE SUGGESTIONS FROM ITS PATRONS CONCERNING ITS SERVICE

CHAPTER 5

ON THE GO

Dad's business took him all over the world in search of ways to make or invest money. Some were trips he initiated, others were on demand from his "kids" who were filming on location or making appearances and wanted him to show up. They needed their business manager to review their ongoing financial situation or to discuss new projects. Isolated from their home base, they predictably got bored or started worrying about their financial state and needed reassurance. Often they got over-enthused about money to be made in real estate or ranches, fishing fleets or oil, lumber mills or crackpot schemes far from home and sent for Dad to come, talk it over, and check it all out. In those days business was basically done on a person-to-person level. Remember that in the '30s, '40s, and '50s we didn't have e-mail, cell phones, answering machines, or fax machines! And "long distance" was a joke, especially when you tried calling abroad or making connections with a film set in a remote location. Meanwhile, decisions had to be made and problems had to be solved. Travel was the way to go. On top of that, most of Dad's clients enjoyed each other's and his company, and combining business with pleasure was a lot of fun. This did not always sit well with wives, girlfriends, or office staff who were sure there was a lot of fooling around going on when everybody was out of town, which was often and most likely true!

In addition, many of our clients took their families with them on location. For instance, John Wayne had many family members on the set when he filmed *The Alamo* and when he filmed *The Quiet Man* in Ireland with John Ford. In fact, one of the reasons given for Duke's breakup with Pilar was that she was tired of going on location with him.

Eventually Dad's business would take him to many countries, but Mexico, in particular, was a fertile ground. Dad and John Wayne loved fishing there on their yacht the *Norwester*, which they owned jointly for a long time. They loved the country, its customs, the people, and the laid-back way of life. Both were hardworking men and needed a chance to relax. Being outgoing people, their idea of relaxation didn't mean sitting in the sun. Instead, they loved to party, and the Mexicans paid back their affection. It also was a convenient (and cheaper) place to put up family and friends, as well as journalists and business people they were trying to cultivate.

Business-wise, Mexico was close to the States, underdeveloped, and eager for American investment and tourists. There were tax advantages to be had. If you went to Mexico as a tourist to play, it was not deductible. But if you went to check on an investment, you could keep sailing, partying, carousing, and "making contacts," and write it all off as a business expense. Dad could find deductions south of the border, as well as north of the border.

Around 1950 Dad was a guest columnist for Pepe Romero in an English-language Mexican newspaper. Dad wrote, "You have made me think of the business side of Mexico. An American gets more for his dollar in Mexico than anywhere in the world ... I would say your identical accommodations are one-half the cost of Rome, Paris and London hotels and restaurants."

I often heard Dad and Duke say they would like to have had dual citizenships for the United States and Mexico. That was not just a personal sentiment. It was sound business judgment. As dual citizens they would have been freer in their dealings in Mexico than they could be as "gringos," since Mexico had limits on many foreign investments. According to Duke's daughter Aissa's account in her book, *John Wayne, My Father*, Duke was seriously considering moving to Mexico in 1978.

Dad's interest in Mexico was widespread. Hedda Hopper wrote from Mexico City that Dad was "a big man down here. Some believe he has the exclusive rights to a lush island not far from town on which he plans to build a casino comparable to Monte Carlo. The way he gets around here is amazing. Everyone associated with him seems to drive a Cadillac."

The Mexican town Dad was most associated with was Acapulco, which brings me to the story of Hotel Los Flamingos, his Mexican base of operations for years. According to my mother's diary, "In 1939 Bö bought the Los Flamingos Hotel in Acapulco with six other men—Fred MacMurray, Rex Allen, John Wayne, Johnny Weissmuller, Frank Belcher and Frank Borzage." Eventually Dad bought out Belcher and Rex Allen. There were limits on Americans owning property in Mexico, so the hotel was purchased by using a Mexican citizen, Carlos Reyes, as a participant. Duke and Dad had a lifelong bond with Carlos that was solidified when Duke was in a local bar once, and a man took out a gun to hold him up. Carlos grabbed the man's arm and nabbed him. After that, Carlos always drove Duke and Dad whenever they were in Mexico.

The hotel was bought as a getaway. In her autobiography *John Wayne—My Life With the Duke,* Pilar Wayne (Duke's third wife) wrote about Dad's "bad deals," including "an Acapulco hotel which stayed so full of nonpaying friends that it never made a profit." Pilar and Duke were married on November 1, 1954, fifteen years after Duke, Dad, and the others bought the place. Initially, making a profit was not the main goal. It was more like a vacation home or private club for friends.

Incidentally, Duke's son Michael wrote off the Los Flamingos after both Dad and Duke had died, mainly because of the complication of the ownership and Mexican laws. My husband, Ted, and I eventually found a buyer, and we were able to sell it and distribute money back to Duke's estate and to Fred MacMurray.

*John Wayne with two marlin and a faded autograph
to me inscribed "Carolyn, you're my gal".*

Wayne, Duke Woods, (Dad's driver and major domo), Dad and
Carlos Reyes (who always drove Dad and John Wayne when
they were in Mexico) showing off their catch in Acapulco.

There was a slight delay until Carlos Reyes found the papers under his wife's bed. Los Flamingos was small. When Dad and his friends bought it, it had only twenty-eight rooms, and it now has only forty-six rooms. Built on one of the highest cliffs in town, it was about 500 feet above the sea with a magnificent view of the ocean. Its signature color was and is an eye-popping pink, reminiscent of flamingos.

The former manager, Adolfo Santiago, is the current owner. When I looked the hotel up on the Internet, I found this message: "Welcome to our family! My home is your home. You dear guest are the reason of our happiness. Enjoy any of our guest rooms in a tropical atmosphere where you can admire wonderful sunsets from your terrace ... Our bar, famous since the '50s for its creation of the Coco Loco, is renown[ed] all over the world ... our prestigious cuisine is well known and highly recommended by local and foreign visitors since 1936."

As Mike Oliver wrote in an *Acapulco Weekly Guide*, Dad and his attorney Frank Belcher took vacations in the month of November, and "with these two live-wires down, we will be seeing some of their important friends ... they get on long distant (sic) and start inviting people to visit them, and nine out of ten follow. Bö and Frank are annual visitors and pioneers of this resort."

When they bought Los Flamingos, Acapulco was a sleepy town. In 1931 the population was only 3,000. By 1947 it was 28,000, which climbed to 100,000 in the early '50s and '60s. Currently it's more than 2 million, and Acapulco is considered the largest and most spectacular tourist resort on the Pacific coast of Mexico.

Dad was nicknamed the "Aga Khan of Acapulco," and a friend gave him bright pink business cards with that name on it so he could hand them out to everybody. The press also called him "The Mayor of Acapulco" because he was always promoting the city. In his guest column for Pepe Romero he described Acapulco as "a play place ... with the wonderful hotels, food and nightclubs, far and above exceeds any other playground so easily accessible to

An original brochure for the Los Flamingos Hotel, in Acapulco, Mexico, showing that reservations were made through Beverly Management Corporation.

Americans. Fishing, the water skiing, and the facilities for fun which are available and the wonderful swimming at Caleta all are gaining world wide recognition and I believe in the year to come and possibly the 1952 season, will show you some new heights in tourist travel from the States." The flight from Los Angeles to Acapulco took only six hours.

Columnist (not the comedian) Rodney Dangerfield in his column "Doin' the Town" wrote that Los Flamingos was a "charming hotel with the Country Club atmosphere and sits atop a hill overlooking the beautiful blue Pacific and Acapulco Bay ... It's considered one of the finest locations in the area ... naturally the music of the mariachis was everywhere and we were handed a Margarita before we had a chance to sit down ... the place was packed and they had to lock the front door to keep people from coming in."

Society columnist Cobina Wright wrote, "Acapulco rivals the French Riviera as a glamour resort, with visitors from all over the world vacationing there. Prince Bernhard of The Netherlands was the incentive for many parties, including one hosted by Bö Roos where Dolores del Rio 'heaven's gift to Mexico' attended."

One of the big attractions then and to this day are the cliff divers at La Quebrada, an exhibition that started in 1934. Divers plunge off a high cliff into twelve feet of water in the ocean below. Mistakes can be fatal. The divers' lives depend on their knowledge of the tides. They don't just dive; some of them do double back flips and twirl flaming torches. It's a skill and talent passed down through generations, and one diver claims to have made almost 40,000 dives over the years. It's a spectacular sight that everybody in town enjoyed seeing over and over, especially since we knew many of the divers. We'd take visiting guests to see them and pose for pictures.

La Perla, the restaurant that was associated with the spectacle, is where I first saw Harry Belafonte. It was a popular rendezvous, as were many bars across town where the drinks were an opener for relaxing, seeing and being seen, flirting, gossiping, and getting

Adolfo Santiago strumming his guitar (with Ted and I looking on)
before he worked his way up to the job of manager of the Los Flamingos
Hotel... The hotel became a popular place for the Hollywood crowd.

caught up in the events of the day. Happy hour in Acapulco seemed to start early and end late. Like most of the bars, Los Flamingos had its powerful signature concoction called the Coco Loco, which contained tequila, gin, and white rum and was served in a coconut shell.

The person who probably did the most to promote Acapulco's growth was President Miguel Alemán, who was in office from 1946 to 1952. He was a great friend of Dad's and his cronies. He and some of his cabinet members built their summer homes in Acapulco, and his yacht *Sotavento* was moored there. That probably helped inspire the government to pave existing roads in the whole town and construct a four-lane boulevard from one end of Acapulco Bay to the other and a connecting road to the airport.

Alemán was also instrumental in establishing the annual Film Review Festival, which was held in Acapulco for thirteen years. The Mexican government invited and paid all the expenses for international stars, costars, directors, producers, distributors, and journalists. As I remember, it was sort of like the Cannes Film Festival. It was hoped that the event would attract more filming in Mexico and greater distribution of Mexican films all over the world. Interest in the Mexican film industry did not escalate, but the bright side was that the Festival was a terrific vehicle

Dad and friend with journalist Mike Oliver (holding champagne bottle) who chronicled the doings in Acapulco for decades.

for promoting tourism. After Alemán left office, he created the National Tourist Council, thereby capitalizing on his vision, though perhaps not in the way he had planned it originally.

Needless to say, Dad was in his element at the film festivals since he knew everybody and was a good friend of Alemán's. Dad was a master at seeing to it that his clients were showcased, networking, and making contacts. He was always good for a story himself. The Hotel Los Flamingos became known as the Hotel of the Stars because Dad was always trailing a bunch of film industry people in his wake and would be sure everyone was available for photos and interviews. The journalists liked him, and he was good at making their lives easier. For instance, he introduced Mike Oliver, publisher of the *Acapulco News*, to many prominent guests, including journalist Bill Kennedy (Mr. L.A.), who feted Mike when he visited Los Angeles. Dad always put Mike up at the Bryson Hotel and Apartments at no charge.

The list of people who visited Acapulco was endless, and since I was there sporadically, I can't recall which ones came while Dad was there and which came later. But I do remember being with

Dad in the middle (as usual) of a bunch of guys having fun and, of course, a bevy of good looking women.

Ted and I with Allene and Johnny Weissmuller and friends in Acapulco.

Rory Calhoun and Lita Baron in the middle, with Dad
and friends on the beach in Acapulco, Mexico.

Duke, Red, Ray Milland, Frank Borzage, Johnny Weissmuller, and Ward Bond as they drank, played cards, told stories, and razzed each other into the night at the Hotel Los Flamingos. On the street, you'd bump into the likes of Bing Crosby, Rock Hudson, Stefanie Powers, and Lana Turner. You'd read in the newspaper about Liz Taylor's getting married to Mike Todd with Eddie Fisher and Debbie Reynolds as witnesses. (Ironic that after Todd's death, Fisher became another of Liz's eight husbands.) Rita Hayworth and then husband Orson Welles would be arriving to film *Lady of Shanghai*. Sinatra would once again be declared "persona non grata" in Mexico. Jayne Mansfield would be busting out all over, to the delight of the photographers. Jackie and John F. Kennedy honeymooned there, as did Linda Christian and Tyrone Power. The list of tourists went on through athletes (Ilie Nastase and Rocky Marciano) and writers (Tennessee Williams, Budd Schulberg, James Michener, Leon Uris, and Harold Robbins). I would have liked to have seen Jimmy Hoffa and his entourage of sixty-nine lawyers for the Teamsters there for their annual

Mom and Dad in Honolulu with Duke Kahanamoku,
winner of two gold medals for swimming in the 1912 and
1920 Olympics and a much loved figure in Hawaii.

meeting! On a bizarre note, Howard Hughes spent his last days at a hotel in Acapulco before he was flown to Houston, where he died, a sad wreck of the man he had been.

I was always fascinated by the yachts that sailed into the harbor. John Wayne's second yacht, the *Wild Goose,* was a converted 136-foot naval minesweeper with twin 500-horsepower engines that is now docked close to my home in Newport Beach, California. Whenever the *Goose* came into sight, you could hear the other boats blow their foghorns in salute. (Previously Duke had owned the *Norwester* with Dad, and later my husband, Ted, and I became its owners.)

Queen Elizabeth arrived in Acapulco on the royal yacht. Prince Charles came on a British navy training ship. Errol Flynn was raising hell on and off his yacht *Sirocco.* Mike Oliver, who saw the yachts come in over his forty-plus years publishing the *Acapulco News* newspaper, thought the most beautiful yacht, the

Dad on a sideline trip in Egypt, on his way to Africa to join with Prince Bernhard of the Netherlands on a Safari. (Did I say this chapter was "On The Go".... right!)

Angelita, was that of General Ramfis Trujillo, the playboy son of the Dominican Republic's president. After Trujillo Sr. was assassinated, Mike reported in his book, *Mike Oliver's Acapulco*, that Ramfis loaded all the gold bars from the treasury aboard the *Angelita*, but it was not fast enough to outrun the Dominican navy, which recovered the loot. Another spectacular yacht Mike recalled was the *Dangin*, owned by Daniel and Ginger Keith with a crew of twenty-four German sailors and a captain who had skippered a U-boat in World War II.

* * * *

In spite of their differences, my parents enjoyed traveling together over the years. Mother enjoyed the V.I.P. treatment and the fact that Dad was paying attention to her. Dad was always curious about seeing new things and meeting new people. Usually, the trips were business related. Sometimes my brother and I went with them.

In 1948 they took my brother to England with them for Johnny Weissmuller's water show, with a stop in Paris and Montmartre. My brother remembers that part of what made their trip significant was that they rendezvoused in Paris with our client director Frank Borzage, winner of two Academy Awards. Frank's film career had spanned the silent era from the early 1900s all the way through the '50s, from 1916's *Life's Harmony* to *China Doll* in 1958. He won two Oscars for directing *Seventh Heaven* and *Bad Girl*. In 1926 Louis B. Mayer called him "one of the towers of strength in the film industry." The French are known for being film buffs and as a result treated them royally along the way. Frank was only ten years older than Dad, and his parents were Swedish, as was my father's dad, so they had a lot in common.

* * * * *

Another time a whole group of friends, including conductor David Rose and his wife, Betty, journalist Gene Fowler, Red Skelton and his wife Georgia, and Mom and Dad, went to Europe on a jaunt before Red did his show at the London Palladium.

Betty Rose remembers Dad and Red racing through the streets of Rome in a chariot. I don't know the details, but I wouldn't put it past the two of them to do something crazy like that.

After spending a few days sightseeing in Italy, they boarded a flight to England. Just after they passed Mont Blanc, two of the plane's engines shut off, and the third one was sputtering. The priest on board had everyone praying while Red entertained the children to keep them calm. Somehow the plane limped into the airport at Lyons, France. It turned out to be a case of sabotage stemming from troubles in the oil fields in Nairobi, where the flight had originated.

The next day a plane was sent from London to pick them up. The landing field was a little short for the size of the plane, and when the pilot landed, the plane's tail swung around into a field of clover. My mother thought the fragrance was lovely and told everyone to "Smell the clover!" Georgia Skelton laughed and said, "We almost crashed, and Billie is smelling the clover!" My father stayed calm but loved that the press picked up on Red's antics in the sky, helping publicize his upcoming London engagement. Gene Fowler was quoted by Hedda Hopper as saying, "Red's butt is still in a sore state; he almost sat down on an Alp."

Red Skelton spent a month at the Palladium in London to smashing reviews and box office sellouts. During that time my parents slipped out for a side trip to Stockholm to visit with friends and relatives.

When Red finished entertaining the Brits, my mother talked everyone into taking the 723-foot luxury liner S.S. *America* home. Judging from the food alone, the voyage was pretty ritzy. I have a menu from about that time that included a marvelous assortment of traditional fare, gourmet staples such as Bluepoint Oysters on the Half Shell, Beluga Malossal Caviar on Ice, Foie Gras, and Gaspe Salmon, plus unusual items such as Purple Partridge, Adirondack Venison, and Braised Ox Tongue. It was a smooth sail for an Atlantic crossing except for one day of bad weather. Red Skelton, always the clown, came to my parents' stateroom green at the gills. They thought he must have eaten something to cause the green and felt sorry for him until they realized that the green color on his "gills" came from Georgia's eye shadow.

* * * * *

In 1962 my parents had a memorable trip when the U.S. Department of Defense invited two prominent businessmen and their wives from each state to tour the important military bases in the Pacific. Dad was obviously a prominent Californian, and he was thrilled to be included.

Their first stop was Hawaii, where they revisited the grim reminders of World War II. They were once again moved by the sight of the battleship *Arizona,* which was sunk by the Japanese and cost 1,176 Americans their lives.

In the Philippines they were taken to an airplane carrier and sailed past Corregidor and out into the ocean, escorted by two destroyers. (Corregidor was an island fortress at the tip of Bataan with concrete tunnels, artesian wells, and heavy guns built to defend the entrance to Manila Harbor, and was yet another reminder of the devastation of war.) There was a demonstration of planes landing and taking off the carrier, and they saw some antisubmarine warfare maneuvers.

In Korea they felt the evidence of yet another war—the Korean War, which lasted from June 25, 1950, to July 27, 1953. They were taken up a hill in a tank, six at a time, where the military showed them how men, jeeps, and small tanks were airlifted during the fighting. A few bombs were also dropped, something the civilians had never experienced. At the 38th parallel they could look into the windows of a building where a meeting was going on between U.S. and North Korean officers while North Korean soldiers patrolled the line just the other side of the building. Mother got very nervous when she found out about a news item that appeared in the Korean press, warning the South Koreans against the group's visit and advising them to "chase us into the sea."

* * * * *

One of the places Dad visited was much closer to home— Camp Pendleton, about 100 miles from Los Angeles, where John Wayne shot one of his most famous movies, *Sands of Iwo Jima.* I remember Dad talking about how Duke really got into his role, which would earn him an Academy Award nomination.

The movie was made with total cooperation from the Marines, who provided troops, equipment, and technical advice. Being a superpatriot, Duke was in his element not only portraying them but in expressing his admiration for their bravery. *Sands of Iwo Jima* was a megahit that is still shown on television today. I remember Dad went to the premiere with Duke, kleig lights piercing the sky and 500 marines parading by with a 150-piece band from Camp Pendleton. What an impressive sight!

Years later, Dad, Mother, and my husband, Ted (who had started as an ensign in the navy and became a commander), talked about their trip to World War II war zones, and what a unique experience it was to have seen a demonstration of warfare firsthand, reliving history where it happened. They also recalled the many movies Duke made with a military theme, including *Back to Bataan*, *The Fighting Seabees*, and *The Green Berets*.

* * * * *

Mom and I enjoying dinner out with Red Skelton. (We were on the go at home while Dad was on the go wherever!)

Lupe Velez surrounded by admirers, as usual. Her popularity in Mexico was second only to Greta Garbo's.

CHAPTER 6

LUPE VELEZ, TOO YOUNG TO DIE

upe Velez was a petite Latin beauty who was all the things my father loved in a client—colorful, challenging, spirited, fun to be with, headline making, passionate, exciting, bubbly. And she drove him crazy in more ways than one—personally and professionally.

She was called "The Mexican Hurricane," "Whoopee Lupe," and "The Hot Tamale." Being born during a hurricane in San Luis de Potosi, Mexico, may have contributed to her volatile temper. By the time she was sixteen, she was performing in a musical revue for $350 a week. In his book *Moving Pictures*, Budd Schulberg claimed her debut was made in burlesque and that she supplemented her income through trysts with amorous men. Who knows if it was true? All the witnesses are dead, and if anything, Lupe attracted rumors and gossip all her life.

Hollywood called when she was seventeen, but immigration authorities wouldn't let her cross the border. When she finally arrived, she claimed she was robbed of all her pesos. Even worse, the studio said she looked too young for the role they had planned for her—not an auspicious start. Her first decent role was in a 1927 Laurel & Hardy short. Her second was playing in *The Gaucho*, opposite Douglas Fairbanks, who was married to Mary Pickford at the time. Reportedly, sparks flew as Fairbanks and his leading lady became attracted romantically while Pickford, "America's

Mom and Dad celebrating a birthday with Lupe Velez and Art LaShelle.

Sweetheart," fumed with jealousy. When the film premiered on November 24, 1927, Lupe received good reviews, as did the new process of Technicolor, which was used in some of the scenes. The studio was thrilled with the film's prospects and charged $1.50 a ticket, six times the normal price. In 1929 she starred in her first talking picture, *Tiger Rose,* with Rin-Tin-Tin, whose movies were so successful he kept his studio from going bankrupt. During her career she appeared in musical revues and on Broadway, had Cole Porter write songs for her, performed with Jimmy Durante and John Barrymore, and captured the American market as well as Latin America, where her popularity was second only to Greta Garbo's.

Her most famous role was as the "Mexican Spitfire" in a series of eight movies starting in 1939 and going through 1942. The stories were trite, but her earthy personality made it all worthwhile for her fans, who were enthralled by her beauty, comedic skills, singing voice, and how she stood up to her leading men. She was constantly in the headlines with her off-screen antics, and nothing made bigger headlines than Lupe's marriage to Johnny Weissmuller from 1933 to 1938.

Johnny was also a client of Dad's, who managed his financial affairs for more than thirty years. I wrote an article in *The Avalon Bay News* in 1993 about him. He was voted the World's Greatest Swimmer of the First Half Century, 1900–1950, by the Sports Writers of America, was a five-time Olympic Gold Medal winner, established sixty-seven world records, and won fifty-two national championships. Johnny taught my brother and me to swim. He also taught my son Jon to swim in the 1950s. However, he did not have the same patience with Jon as he did with us, so he just picked Jon up and threw him in the pool. I nearly had a heart attack, but to this day Jon is still a good swimmer.

I knew Johnny was Tarzan when I went to the movies, but he was just "Johnny" to me and my family. He starred in eighteen Tarzan films from 1931 to 1947, attracting audiences with his buffed body, good looks, athleticism, skimpy loincloth, trademark Tarzan yell, and dialogue as simple as "Me Tarzan, you Jane." (Supposedly when he was offered the role, Johnny said, "Me? Tarzan?") Johnny was handsome, charming, and more than popular with the ladies.

Two gorgeous and successful stars living in Lupe's large, elegantly furnished home, the Casa Felicitas (Happy Home), in the heart of Beverly Hills, with a huge swimming pool in the back yard for Johnny to work out in would seem to be ideal. They were also both highly sexed. Johnny once flaunted his "manhood" in front of my father and brother—and Lupe. Tallulah Bankhead, who claimed 180 sexual conquests at one point (I wonder how

Lupe Velez and Beryl Weissmuller and Dad in the middle, as usual...
between an ex-wife and the third wife of Johnny Weissmuller.

she kept track), recalled an encounter with Johnny at the Garden of Allah pool and reported she had been "a very satisfied Jane."

You would think that their marriage would have been made in heaven, but each had a fiery temperament, and their fights were constant. The word "tempestuous" is hardly adequate to describe their relationship.

Columnist Paul Coates interviewed Dad and Weissmuller once at the California Country Club. He quoted Dad as saying that Lupe and Johnny would "call me up in the middle of the night, whenever they had a fight." She'd swear she was going to "keel heem or deevorce heem." Dad would drive over and spend the night trying to restore peace, with six yipping Chihuahuas running around the room. The police were called more than once.

Many fights culminated with Lupe locking Johnny out of the bedroom. Coates said Johnny added proudly, "And I'd always bust down the door." Dad added that "She was always locking him in or out of the house. Their biggest household expense was Yale locks!" Dad said, "Crazy temper but that girl has a heart of gold."

Johnny claimed that "The only way I could quiet her down was to smash one of her antiques. That used to break her spirit. But I had to learn to be a collector before I knew what vases were worth smashing." My mother remembered when Lupe had a cabinet full of beautiful collectible ivory figurines. One day her housekeeper was dusting and knocked down an ivory elephant, breaking off its trunk. Lupe was very superstitious and insisted that the broken trunk meant bad luck and had the cabinet and contents removed from the house that day.

Lupe *did* love gold in all its forms, but she also loved diamonds, rubies, and emeralds. One of her emerald-cut diamonds was twenty carats. Her signature was a collection of gem-encrusted bracelets, each at least an inch wide. She wore them at least four at a time, wrist to elbow, dazzling her fans and the cameras. Her clothes were gorgeous, and I was told she had one of the first chinchilla coats ever made in the United States. I've seen a lot of jewelry on movie stars since then, but nobody I can think of could match her dazzle. Another favorite possession of hers was a yellow Dusenberg, trimmed in black, with doors faced with rattan. You can imagine why the press loved her for always giving them something to write about or to photograph. Her romantic escapades before and after Johnny just spiced the whole thing up.

When Lupe asked Dad to be her business manager, she was more than $50,000 in debt, and her spending habits kept escalating. Dad shepherded her finances, and at one point he arranged for her to borrow money from my grandfather, using her famous gems as collateral.

Weissmuller was not much help when it came to managing their spending sprees. He was quoted in the press, though, as calling my dad "a genius" who prevented him from going broke but kept him on such a tight budget that he "once had to climb through Bö's office window to steal a pink slip so he could get more money" to rescue a bookie in trouble.

In addition to gold, gems, and antiques, Lupe loved plain old cash. She and Dad cared a great deal about each other, but when it came to money, they hardly ever agreed. It wasn't always easy for Dad to try to explain the whys and wherefores of managing her finances. It wasn't just the language barrier. It was much more emotional.

Ella Wickersham, a *Herald Examiner* columnist, described the tense situation when she wrote, "You should really remember Bö Roos in your prayers, for his is the Herculean task of keeping the fiery Lupe Velez under financial control. His nightly dreams are filled with the furs, diamond bracelets and other luxuries that Lupe will spring on him the next day. At the last handicap race at Santa Anita, Lupe had Kayak II right on the nose. So, flushed with extra cash, she went right out and made a down payment on a yacht." Dad called and told me to send the yacht back immediately. He had a big temper, and he was really upset. He yelled, "They've already got a damn yacht. What the hell do they need another one for? Dammit, they can't afford two yachts." I knew that, and I also knew their existing yacht very well. It was a fifty-two-foot sloop named the *Santa Guadalupe* on which we often sailed to Catalina and Mexico.

EXAMINER 1/24/35

Simply laden with diamond bracelets, Lupe Velez arrives at a party with her business manager, B. C. Roos. She wears five bracelets of diamonds and precious stones.

"I've seen the internal revenue man," said Frank Fay when he opened at the Trocadero in "a series of comic concerts and impromptu fun," "and he told me that if I work steadily through 1940, '41 and '42, that I would be even with the Government for 1935, '36 and '37. So just remember, if you should hiss or throw anything, you won't be attacking me, but insulting the Stars and Stripes, for I'm not working for Fay, but the U. S. A."

Fay, however, was in his usual excellent form and the dignity of the nation was hilariously preserved. And ringsiders who turned out for this revival of the famed Sunday night shows at the Troc were Lupe Velez with her business manager, Bo Roos; George Raft and Mack Gray with a party, Mary Livingstone and Jack Benny, Lana Turner and Greg Bautzer, Bob Burns, Harry Joe Brown, the Ralph Murphys, the Charles Biglows, J. Carroll Naish, Joe Pasternak and Edward Ludwig.

A not very clear newspaper article showing Lupe clubbing with Dad and showing off her signature collection of diamond and gem encrusted bracelets which she wore four or five at a time. Her estate valued them at over $100,000 (way back then).

Lupe especially loved people, and people loved her, from the lowest classes to the highest. Some of her most devoted fans shared her love of boxing at the Hollywood Legion Stadium and came to watch her yell and scream as much as they came for the fights in the ring. Once she got so excited, she swung her purse through the ropes from ringside at one of the fighters, nearly knocking him out.

If she was a hit in America, her Mexican fans were even more devoted. My parents went to Mexico with her when she did the picture *La Sandungo*. So many of her fans were at the train that the police had to rescue her by taking her to the hotel on the back of a motorcycle. Even then her clothes were torn. On the way to Mexico City on a train, the motorman stopped at every little village so she could appear on the platform on the last car to greet her fans.

I knew, of course, that Dad was more than a little infatuated with Lupe. He had said, "With Lupe, every night is Saturday night." She accompanied him often when he "did the rounds" as he called it, which was nightclubbing with clients to the most glamorous clubs of the day. Dad said he had to help his clients keep their names in the limelight. With Lupe, he also did a little gambling in the back rooms of a couple of the clubs. I'd often see their pictures and names in the trades and gossip columns the next day in close conversation at Ciro's, dancing the night away.

Her romantic entanglements before and after her marriage to Weissmuller read like a who's who of Hollywood. Gary Cooper was supposedly the love of her life, but she proved to be too much for him. It was reputed that she took a shot at him from a pistol for breaking up with her and that he suffered a nervous breakdown from too much Lupe. She also had liaisons with John Gilbert, Randolph Scott, Tom Mix, Clark Gable, Charlie Chaplin, Red Skelton, Erich Maria Remarque, Errol Flynn, and many more. According to Michael Freedland in his book, *The Two Lives of Errol Flynn*, Errol thought "she had one considerable attribute, the ability to make her breasts dance independently of

Johnny and Lupe on a good day.

each other." Kenneth Anger in *Babylon II* called her men "a small army of lovers."

It all ended on the night of December 14, 1944. Lupe's housekeeper called to tell Dad that something was terribly wrong. Dad rushed over to her house and called me to come over. When I got there, I could see my dad's car, next to police cars and an ambulance with lights flashing. I passed the medics carrying Lupe's body down the stairs, a scarf covering her face. I knew she was gone.

I could feel tears welling up, and when I went in, I could tell Dad had been crying, too. We just stood with our arms around each other for the longest time. Then he told me what had happened.

He had gone into Lupe's bedroom and seen that there were flowers all around and lots of candles still lighted. It was like a scene from a movie set. She had staged it all for a Lothario who had gotten her pregnant but wouldn't marry her. Dressed in a glamorous negligee, she had taken pills either to calm herself or to scare him. He never showed. Rather than being found with her beautiful dark hair spread over the satin pillowcases surrounded by her lovely antiques, Lupe Velez had gotten sick to her stomach, gone into the bathroom to throw up, and died on the cold tile floor next to the toilet, alone. She was only thirty-six.

When Lupe had told Dad of her situation, he had arranged for her to go to Mexico and stay at his Los Flamingos Hotel until the baby was born. Being a Catholic, abortion was out of the question. One of Lupe's sisters in Mexico City would take care of the baby.

Later, Lupe could go back to Mexico and "adopt" the baby. The rumor in Hollywood was that Gary Cooper was the father, not the Lothario. The story of Lupe's death is still clouded by rumors and suspicions. Many of them resulted because Dad had asked the Beverly Hills police chief, a friend of his, to help put a lid on the story. But what I've reported is what my father told me, and I have no reason to disbelieve him.

In his biography *Tarzan, My Father*, Johnny Weissmuller Jr. wrote that the stories of Lupe's death are many and varied and that nobody seemed to know the details. He added: "Bill Reed (his co-author) was fortunate enough to talk with Bö Roos's daughter, Carolyn Roos Olsen, recently, and she gave him the ... account of the death of Lupe Velez, which I am convinced is pretty accurate."

He also said that after Lupe's death his father told him he "thought often about that conversation they'd had at Toots Shor's back in 1939, when Lupe had said, 'Poor John-ee. You do not know that peace comes only in the grave.'" His dad called Lupe "a sad and tormented woman."

Lupe's death broke Dad's heart. After all the glamour and fire, handling her marriage problems, and arranging a cover-up for her pregnancy, there could not help but be a depth of feeling. He had fixed her finances, too. When she died in 1944, her estate was worth about a quarter million dollars with all her debts and taxes paid. Dad had lost a beloved person in his life. Lupe was buried in Mexico in a private plot. The Catholic Church considered her death a suicide and would not approve her being buried in consecrated ground in a Catholic cemetery. Dad told me he had a beautiful monument made for her and hired a gardener to keep flowers on her grave every day for as long as he lived and to pass the job on to someone else to keep it going forever.

Mother, who must have suspected the extent of Dad and Lupe's relationship, was gracious, as always. She donated a couple of beautiful gowns Lupe had given her to a Mexican museum and at their request, wrote these lines about Lupe to accompany the exhibit:

"Lupe was a charming person with a great sense of comedy. At times her language was a bit naughty, but she was far from being alone in that. Never did she say anything out of line when my children were with her ... She was a wonderful person to have as a friend, thoughtful, and so much fun to be with. We all had many happy times together. She will live long in our memories."

Jimmy Durante had called Lupe "a female Pagliacci" with a dark, sad side.

She was not alone. Suicide was a solution to romantic problems for more than one star, including another client of Dad's, the beautiful blonde Carole Landis. Columnist and F. Scott Fitzgerald's mistress Sheilah Graham wrote in her book, *Hollywood Revisited*, "I remember how Lilli Palmer stood by Rex Harrison when Carole Landis took an overdose of pills in 1948 after she realized that Rex was not going to divorce Lilli to marry her." Carol was only twenty-nine, and had already had four unhappy marriages and a string of sad affairs.

Sheilah also remembered when Rachel Roberts, the fourth Mrs. Harrison, decided to ruin his opening night for the touring company of *My Fair Lady* in San Francisco by committing suicide. When they told Rex, he said, "I'm not surprised. I always thought she would do it."

Lupe greeting fans on a train in Mexico, with my Mom at her side.

Walter Huston, who starred in the film *Kongo* with Lupe, says a line in the film *Dodsworth*, "... love has to stop somewhere short of suicide." For more than one star, suicide was the bitter end to love. In contrast, another point of view was exhibited by Katharine Hepburn. Someone claimed that she had wanted to commit suicide over her affair with Howard Hughes. One of Hepburn's close friends was astonished. "Kate Hepburn commit suicide over a man? Murder maybe, but *never* suicide."

Johnny Weissmuller's career as Tarzan was followed by sixteen Jungle Jim films, a stint on television, and promotional appearances. His spendthrift ways and financial troubles followed him throughout his life. (See Chapter 13 "Sticks & Stones" for details.)

His obituary from the Associated Press indicated he had suffered strokes in the 1970s and "was hospitalized at the Motion Picture and Television Country Hospital. After the director there complained that his Tarzan calls in the middle of the night disturbed other patients, Weissmuller and his (fifth) wife moved to a house in Acapulco where he died" at the age of seventy-nine. According to Johnny Weissmuller Jr.'s book *Tarzan, My Father*, he died "a lonely and broken man." I like to remember him as a dear person in his glory days.

Bö, Duke and Los Angeles County Supervisor Leonard Roach harmonizing in the good old days… "Friends were dearer then, too bad we had to part."

CHAPTER 7

JOHN WAYNE, OUR CLIENT & FRIEND

More than nineteen books are *currently* in print about John Wayne. Dozens more were written before and have been written since his death in 1979, some by people who didn't know him at all. Some are based on hearsay; others are strictly sensational cut-and-paste jobs from the tabloids and fan magazines. A few are totally untrue and borderline libelous in what they say about my father. I've written only about what I saw and knew firsthand about Duke as a client and one of Dad's best friends for many fun-filled years.

Dad and Duke's relationship went far beyond business. They had similar backgrounds and were born only four years apart. Even their horoscopes meshed. I have an old horoscope birthday book that captures the two men's personalities to a tee. With descriptions such as these, no wonder I think there is something to horoscopes.

John Wayne was born on May 26, 1907. He was depicted this way: "You have a sunny disposition, dislike ease and idleness, and are always on the go. You are quick-tempered and sometimes brutally frank in speech. You like many people around you. You are very generous and like to entertain others at your expense."

My dad's birthday was October 30, 1903, and he was described as follows: "You have an alert, shrewd mind and a dominating manner which influences others. You are self-confident and very

Dad and Duke enjoying a break from fishing,
swimming and general mischief in Acapulco.

capable. You are stubborn and accustomed to having your own
way. Marry young and choose an amiable, loving mate."

Both came from poor families and worked hard all their lives.
Duke's father had been given a diagnosis of tuberculosis, which
prompted the family's move to California. When Granddad
Holmes suspected he had TB, he also moved his family west. Each
of them delivered newspapers when they were little, Bö at the age
of seven or eight, Duke at age eleven. Duke applied to the U.S.
Naval Academy at Annapolis. Dad's brother Ed made contacts to
get Bö into the Naval Academy.

Together, Duke and Dad invested, partied, and traveled, and
were kindred spirits throughout. Both liked to sail, hunt, fish,
drink, and play poker and gin rummy. They both loved Mexico,
especially Acapulco, which Dad believed would become a major
tourist resort and offered great opportunities for investment. They
liked the Mexican people, the scenery, the music, and the laid-
back style of living. Their friendship and lifestyle caused stress
in my parents' marriage, as well as Duke's. The men were staying
home less in the evenings and going out of town a lot together
with friends and Dad's other clients. It caused problems, but "the

Carlos Reyes, Dad, Duke and a friend in Mexico City.

boys" continued to do what they damned well pleased.

As far as dealing with John Wayne was concerned, I learned quickly not to try to tell him **no!** I tried. As John Wayne's business manager, my father tried. A lot of people did. We all found out it not only wasn't easy, but could be dangerous and was definitely not productive.

If you ever saw Duke on screen taking a "no" from somebody, you could be sure sparks would fly and heavy words would be spoken. When Maureen O'Hara told him "no" in *The Quiet Man*, he dragged her home, kicking and screaming. When Lee Marvin said "no" in *Donovan's Reef*, the whole bar exploded into a brawl. When his leg was broken in *The Longest Day* and he was told he couldn't go on, he had it taped up and barreled on to fight the Nazis.

The fireworks were the same in his real life. The first time I was *personally* involved in trying to say "no" to John Wayne was when he was hell bent on marrying "Chata"—Esperanza Baur Dias Ceballos—a twenty-year-old bit player in Mexican movies and a party girl. Dad had taken Ray Milland, Fred MacMurray, Ward Bond, and Duke on a trip to Mexico to do some fishing, bask in the sun, relax, carouse, play poker, and predictably drink more than they should. It was also a business trip because they were looking into buying the Churubusco Film Studios. Dad invited a group of key people from the Mexican motion picture industry to lunch at a posh club in Acapulco to get acquainted, and, knowing that Duke liked women, had seated him next to Chata. She flirted, he got a kick out of her broken English, and pretty soon Duke was waxing eloquent about how Latin-American women in general and Chata in particular liked the simple things in life such as marriage, family, children, a home. How wrong he was about Chata, but it took years on a roller coaster ride of misery to convince him.

First of all, Duke was already married. He and Josephine Saenz were married in 1933 when John Wayne was still Marion Michael Morrison. Their ten-year marriage had produced four children and

John Wayne swore a lot. My son Denis remembers one day when he was very young watching Dad tending bar at my parent's house, while John Wayne, Johnny Weissmuller and Ward Bond were laughing like crazy. My Mom, 5 ft. in her stocking feet, was pounding on six foot four Duke with her fists, as he apologized, "I guess I'm not supposed to say f*** in front of the kid!"

too many arguments from two people who were temperamentally unsuited. It didn't help that he was so busy at the studios, not coming home, spending time with his pals. Rumors flew, and Josie fumed. Finally, in 1943 she got a legal separation. For two years she didn't speak to Duke or allow him in the house, but being a devout Catholic she didn't believe in divorce either. Her hopes for a reformation for Duke and a reconciliation for the two of them didn't pan out, and after a dispensation from her church, she finally agreed to a divorce, precipitated no doubt by Chata's coming to Hollywood. The divorce was final in 1945. Duke was quoted by Maurice Zolotow in his biography of John Wayne, *Shooting Star*, as saying, "When we split up, I took just one car and my clothes and Josie got all the rest of it, including every cent I had saved." Duke gave her $75,000 plus 20 percent of the first $100,000 of his earnings and 10 percent of everything he earned above this figure to continue as long as she lived. Each child had an individual trust fund. Josie got custody of the children, and Duke got visitation rights.

Meanwhile there was Chata, waiting in the wings. She knew something about the movie business, though she seemed willing to give up her aspirations at acting if it meant being with Duke. She had some spark to her (something he always admired in a woman), liked sports, claimed she liked a home and "could cook a leetle" and garden. He really didn't like being a bachelor. He wanted more children. He was sure they were in love. And so he decided he would marry Chata.

Which resulted in Dad's and my mighty efforts to try to say "no" to John Wayne. They came to my house to talk in private. Dad was in one room yelling at Duke that he already had a wife and four children to support. He couldn't afford any more financial burden. While Dad was twisting Duke's arm in one room and telling him of the financial pitfalls that awaited him, I was in the other room with Chata, telling her it would not be a good idea to marry a man with so many family and financial obligations. We brought up the fourteen-year age difference. I told her Duke was a man's man and wasn't a stay-at-home type, no matter what he said. On top of that, both Dad and I knew that Chata's mother had been a "lady friend" to some very important men in Mexico and had brought Chata up to follow in her footsteps. Josie was a lady; Chata wasn't. Neither was her mother, who taught her everything she knew. I really couldn't understand what Duke saw in her. Chata sobbed, Dad yelled, I coaxed, and Duke did what he wanted to do in the first place—married Chata in 1946, three weeks after his divorce from Josie was final. We were right; Duke was wrong. When it came time to clean up the mess, we were deeply involved.

Long before the movie *The Alamo*, Duke had his own personal "Alamo" with Chata. He hadn't married the homebody he thought he had. Part of the problem was that Duke had asked Chata's mother to live with them. Both of the women drank, fumed, and egged each other on with their complaints about him. They had expected a life of glamour with a big movie star in the heart of Hollywood. Instead, initially after the divorce from Josie there was little money left for glamour. Duke had to get back to work to support all his dependents. One of Chata's big complaints was that all Duke and his friends talked about was "thee beeziness," that he did not love her or sleep with her, he slept with the pictures. I remember many times with Duke and my dad when they spent the entire evening "cussing and discussing" their many projects. Once in particular I remember going to Chasen's with them, feeling like a star myself with two handsome men on either side of me. I always enjoyed listening to them talking about their activities. It didn't bother me that Duke swore a lot. He just could not converse without a few four-letter words added for effect.

The kinds of fights Chata and Duke had went beyond normal husband-and-wife disagreements. Duke spent a lot of time at my dad's house, commiserating, and Dad spent a lot of time trying to calm things down between them and arranging reconciliations, including a second honeymoon in Hawaii. I remember once Duke and I had lunch together. He had had another fight with

Chata the night before, and she had locked him out of the house, including the security gates. He wanted me to call Chata and ask her to let him back in, and he even got a bit teary eyed when he told me how much he loved her. I simply couldn't see what he saw in the woman. She was difficult, not even pretty, her complexion was always blotchy, and she drank a lot more than she should. But I assured him I'd do the best I could.

As I sat looking at him, I thought how ruggedly handsome he was, and so damn nice. I really loved him and wished he could have stayed married to his first wife, who was such a nice person, a real lady. I understood their marriage had broken up because Josie wasn't interested in the "physical side of marriage," as Duke put it in the divorce proceedings. When the judge pointed out that they had four children, Duke said, "Four times—in ten years." Josie was a very devout Catholic and didn't want more children. She was very involved in Catholic charities, as were Dolores Hope, Irene Dunne, Loretta Young, Mary Ford, and also Ray Milland's wife. I heard Duke complain that their parties were "always ass deep in priests." (When he was married to Chata, even though he loved Mexico and Mexicans, he complained that he was "ass deep in Mexicans" and couldn't understand the Spanish of his wife, her mother, and the non-English-speaking servants they hired.)

In 1951 Chata got a court order barring Duke from their home, saying he had threatened her life. Duke got a court order letting him back in to visit their dog. Duke came "home," fell asleep in a chair, and woke up staring into the barrel of a gun in the hands of a detective Chata had hired to shoot him on sight.

Chata hired famed divorce attorney Jerry Giesler to handle her divorce. (Later Jerome Rosenthal took over from Giesler.) We all wanted to keep the whole thing quiet for the sake of everybody concerned. Duke said he'd accept the accusation of "mental cruelty." Frank Belcher, Duke's attorney, started negotiations. Dad figured out a financial settlement of $325,000 over a nine-year period. Chata's demands were more ambitious, including $12,500 *a month forever*, which she needed for the following:

Household maintenance	$1,245
Household expenses	$1,938
Personal expenses	$3,654
Auto upkeep, traveling	$ 948
Health and insurance	$1,513
Mother's allowance	$ 650
Furs, jewelry, personal effects	$ 499
Charities	$1,023
Travel fares	$ 794
Telephone	$ 301
Personal clothing	$ 746
Gifts	$ 261

Duke was willing to give her what she wanted except for the allowance for his mother-in-law. Dad was adamant that Duke not saddle himself with this kind of burden *for life*!!! Once again he was fighting Duke's "no." We sent a courier to Mexico with $150,000 cash to try to calm Chata down. She kept the money but didn't calm down. She seemed to welcome the ruckus and her opportunity to "tell all" in public. The headlines read, "COULDN'T MAKE ENDS MEET ON $160,000 A YEAR!" while the average American's yearly income at the time was around $4,000.

But a funny thing happened on the way to court. Hampton Scott, who was Duke's butler/chauffeur, gave him a slip of paper that Chata had written showing that Nicky Hilton had spent a week at their house with her while Duke was away on location.

The fight was on, and it got really nasty. Her attorney said, "She was swept into a mode of living where life came from the mouth of a whiskey bottle." She accused Duke of having had an affair with Gail Russell, his costar in *Angel and the Badman*, on the night the production wrapped. Under oath Duke testified in response to his attorney Frank Belcher's question about that evening, "I got home about one-thirty A.M. My wife refused to let

**The John Wayne Case
—Stop, Look and Listen**

Mrs. Esperanza Wayne appears to be giving special attention to her husband, Actor John Wayne (center), as he confers with attorneys during recess in their torrid suit here. Newest "big name" to enter the case is Nicky Hilton, hotel fortune heir. He'll be called to tell about the week he was a guest of Mrs. Wayne while John was away.

—Herald-Express Photo

Wayne divorce hits the papers.

me in. I could hear her and her mother talking about me loudly. I rang the bell but they wouldn't open the door. Then I broke a glass panel, reached in, and opened it myself. Later Chata and her mother, they came charging out. Chata had a .45 in her hand. She and her mother were fighting over it. Then things quieted down."

Quieted down?! The banner headlines on the *Herald Express* newspaper read, "NEARLY SHOT WAYNE AFTER HIS NIGHT OUT, SAYS WIFE." and the *Los Angeles Herald Examiner* reported, "JOHN WAYNE ON STAND, BLASTS BACK AT CHATA." Things didn't quiet down; they kept heating up.

Chata was always accusing Duke of "clobbering" her. In the courtroom screenwriter James Edward Grant testified that Chata once told him, "That son-of-a-bitch hit me" the day before. Grant said it couldn't have been Duke because, "If that is so, it is the longest punch thrown in history, because Duke was up in Moab, Utah, making a picture."

Dad spent a lot of time in court looking after Duke's assets. A settlement was finally reached for a total payment of $450,000. Chata got $150,000 outright, $20,000 for debts, and $50,000 a year for six years, a total of $450,000, 30 percent more than Dad had hoped for.

After the divorce Chata went back to Mexico City. I was told that she had used up the $150,000 cash settlement, was living in a cheap hotel, and drank herself to death, dying of a heart attack within a year.

In 1951 before the fight with Chata was resolved, Duke had traveled to South America courtesy of Howard Hughes and RKO and took a break from domestic problems when he met Pilar Palette Weldy, an actress in Peruvian films. Pilar's marriage was falling apart, and she and Duke fell hard for each other. Shortly thereafter, Harrison Carroll was writing, "Any lingering hope of a reconciliation between the John Waynes was wiped out yesterday with John's return from South America."

I think Duke was a big romantic, always looking for the love of his life and believing that he and a woman could have real companionship. In her autobiography *'Tis Herself*, Maureen O'Hara says the nicest thing Duke ever said to her was, "There's only one woman who has been my friend over the years, and by that I mean a real friend, like a man would be. That woman is Maureen O'Hara. She's big, lusty, absolutely marvelous—definitely my kind of woman ... I prefer the company of men. Except for Maureen O'Hara." Maureen said their onscreen chemistry was so great because he never had to defer to her as a woman. "I was strong enough to stand up to him and be his equal. He used to say that I was the greatest guy he ever knew."

But Maureen wasn't the kind of woman Duke was looking for in his love life. Overlapping the divorce proceedings with Chata was "John Wayne's new romance" Pilar Palette, according to Louella Parsons. Dad had met Pilar and told us she seemed very attractive, very nice, and "very normal." The word around the office was that it looked like Duke had a winner this time. He had tried to bring her up with him when he returned from South America but didn't have the proper paperwork. I was making arrangements for someone to drive down over the weekend to Tijuana to bring her across the border. We all hoped Duke's third marriage would be the charm. His divorce from Chata was final in October 1954. Pilar and Duke were married in Hawaii on November 1. Three children and twenty years later, his marriage to Pilar fell apart with a trial separation.

Duke's personal life was challenging, and we got very involved in it. To keep everybody supported through alimony, divorces, and child support was not easy. You'll see how we tried to do it and carry on his business and ours in the next chapter.

CHAPTER 8

John Wayne –
Money, Money, Money

Duke had been a client since 1941, although he and Dad had met sometime earlier at the Hollywood Athletic Club, where Dad was one of the founders. Marlene Dietrich, another client of ours at the time, had steered Duke to us after she heard his finances were a mess.

Dad and Duke clicked right away. They had a wonderful business relationship for many years. Warren Cowan, who heads one of the most important public relations agencies in Hollywood, told me, "The story I best remember about your father had to do with the Cabana Club, which your father organized with the backing of several of his star clients. Unfortunately, the club came too late. By the time it opened most stars had their own swimming pools and the swimming pool attraction of the club, which would have worked in the '20s and '30s, simply did not work in the '40s. I recall sitting at the club one night with your father and John Wayne. Business was very slow and your father was discussing the fact that the club was in trouble. With that, John Wayne took out his checkbook, handed it to your father, and said, 'Bö, write in any amount that you need to help keep this place going, and I'll sign the check.' I had never seen a gesture that generous. It showed the tremendous faith that John Wayne had in Bö Roos."

Not everybody deserved Duke's faith. I always thought he was an intelligent man, but vulnerable when it came to the really nice guy con man type. He had a lot of what was known as "hangers-on" around the movie business crowd. He enjoyed the company of men, playing bridge, poker, Scrabble, or chess, and drinking and smoking, all in the mode of "hail-fellow-well-met". The only problem was that too many times the hail-fellow had a brother or uncle or friend with some really terrific business deal that shouldn't be passed up. It wasn't very businesslike, but I think he got a kick out of it all. Duke was always optimistic about money. Anytime he was running short, he thought he could solve everything by doing another picture. And for years he was right. When he was making B Westerns, they were churned out at the rate of one a week. I've lost count of the number of films he made over the years.

Maureen O'Hara said he was the hardest-working actor she'd ever been on a picture with. He was always prepared and professional. And although there was a lot of drinking after hours, he could really hold his liquor. Other guys might be hung over, but if he was, he never showed it. He was on the set at six in the morning, knowing his lines and ready to start shooting.

Meanwhile, Duke's star was rising both in the movies and in public opinion. Film historian Leonard Maltin wrote in his *Movie Encyclopedia* that John Wayne had "come to represent the archetypal American of our country's formative period: honest, direct, decisive, solitary and reverent ... whose belief in justice spurs him to right wrongs when they're discovered. John Wayne ... played that character ... in almost every movie he made, and it became so much a part of him that most people couldn't separate the real Wayne from his screen persona." Americans responded, and in 1949, he first appeared on the Top Ten list of movie box office stars, and stayed on the list until 1974 (five years before his death), according to *American Chronicle*.

A lot of money was coming in; unfortunately, it was also seeping out. Maurice Zolotow quoted Dad as saying, "It was impossible to get Duke to stay on a budget ... He just couldn't say no to a guy he liked and, hell, sometimes he wouldn't tell you, wouldn't tell me, or anybody in the office he was signing a check. However, at least (Beverly Management Corporation) did get Wayne's capital invested to some extent." Dad and Duke often argued about how his money should be used.

One major part of Dad's advice to Duke was to organize his own independent production company, and Bob Fellows, Duke's partner at the time, credited Dad with coming up with the idea. Wayne-Fellows Productions, Inc., was a precursor to Batjac, formed in 1954, and was doing very well. At the same time, Duke started thinking about handling all of his business himself through his new company. Dad had discouraged Duke from leaving our office because he thought Duke needed some cool business heads around him. He thought, though, that it was only a matter of time before Duke made the move, and he was worried that Duke would fall prey to a lot of business schemes that Dad was able to deflect.

Duke's relationship with BMC began to crumble in the mid-'50s, about the time he was getting obsessed with making the movie *The Alamo*. He thought it was a great American story that needed to be told and wanted to direct it himself. Everybody told him not to do it. Warner Brothers Studios and Paramount indicated they'd produce it *if* it included a major director, such as John Ford or Howard Hawks. My father rang financial alarm bells on the project. John Ford, who had directed John Wayne in some of his most successful films, thought that Duke was too old, had never directed, and didn't know that much about production, and that it was a very complicated project to use as a learning experience. Family, friends, lawyers, studio executives—everybody tried to dissuade him. Nothing worked. Once again, "no" wasn't in his vocabulary.

In 1958 Duke was in Tokyo, where he was promoting *The Barbarian and the Geisha*. The news clipping I have showed him with what was called his "brain trust" and included Dad, "the star's business manager." That same year Duke terminated his relationship with Beverly Management Corporation.

In 1959 *The Alamo* went into production. Duke wound up getting half the startup money from United Artists on the condition that Batjac put up the other half and John Wayne play Davy Crockett. He got a bunch of Texas oilmen to invest and then mortgaged many of his assets. He said he had "everything he owned in the picture, except his necktie." The movie was the most expensive ever made until that time. It wasn't a blockbuster, and there was a lot of bad publicity. Many critics and people in the industry bashed the film in general and Duke in particular. I've heard that Duke lost almost half a million dollars on the picture.

In her memoir, *John Wayne, My Father*, Aissa Wayne wrote, "... the early '60s were a watershed in my father's personal life ... For it was around this time ... sickness ravaged his patience ... my father lashed out when he felt himself getting weak."

They were all getting older, business was more complicated, and financial demands were getting heavier. It led to Duke and Dad's having their own Alamo when Duke claimed he didn't have any money, blamed Dad for the losses, and threatened to sue. Dad explained that Duke's assets weren't liquid, and that he'd been through a messy and expensive divorce from Chata. He was still supporting a wife and four kids in a style befitting a movie star from his marriage to Josie. He had started another family with Pilar. Dad confided in me that he hadn't been able to keep up with Duke's largesse and over-the-top ideas and advise him how to get enough money to pay for it all.

The dispute led to their agreement to appoint an arbitrator to settle their differences. Howard S. Meighan was named the arbitrator and issued his final decisions in September 1964. He gave the background of the situation as follows: "For nearly twenty years Roos served Wayne as Business Manager. In addition, they were business partners or associates in various deals and warmly affectionate personal friends. On December 27, 1958, Wayne terminated Roos' employment as Business Manager effective

December 31, 1958." The arbitrator complimented and scolded both of them: "... Wayne and Roos are unusual men. Each have monumental assets and each have glaring faults. Each have a unique ability to create complex business and personal problems for themselves. Each have strong emotional motivation which often greatly affects their rational judgment. Each communicated orally by preference and apparently shun or are inexpert in writing techniques. The lack of written communication, on the part of each, is a basic source of their eventual breakup and varying memory as to facts, episodes and understandings. The basic problem of the Arbitrator is to dissect the pertinent history, allocate responsibility and determine the degree, if any, of any overbalancing inequity ...

"What happened to reverse the confidence Wayne had apparently placed in Roos for nearly twenty years? It appears that increasing income tax pressure on increasing gross revenues for personal services drove Wayne and his manager-advisor Roos to seek new systems for preserving his income. Wayne-Fellows, Batjac and the sister or successor corporations were devised to develop capital assets from personal services. But this brought two things, a high operating overhead and an 'inside' Wayne staff. Soon Fellows, Wayne's inside associate, and Roos, his outside associate, were at odds ... then Weesner joined Wayne's inside staff as a financial man. Then Fellows left, LaCava and Newman were added. Unwittingly, Wayne had set up competitive forces among his inside and outside staffs. His long periods of absence while making pictures opened up multiple opportunities for friction and rivalry with no one on top to command. Soon the inside staff was demanding data and reports from Roos ... Meetings required the attendance and help of Arthur Andersen & Co. In effect, this was an expensive education of the inside staff into the unique, complex and interwoven history and affairs of Wayne."

Meighan added, "During 1958 Wayne permitted the responsibility for his affairs to become subtly bifurcated, setting his inside organization and his outside organization in competition for his favor and esteem. The extraordinary services demanded by those who were not previously familiar with the complex background of Wayne's affairs were costly."

Dad had figured out a complex deal called the Jim Wood cotton deal, which had impressed Duke, but the arbitrator wrote, "Despite the fact that it was Roos' deal, Wayne's inside staff wrestled it out of Roos' hands by December, 1958 and took it over. Wayne was busy on location with the *Horse Soldiers*. The competitive situation he had permitted thrived in his absence and finally Wayne's outside staff was defeated. Roos was discharged. It's likely that Wayne has never seen objectively what he permitted to happen with a bifurcated organization."

A major problem area stemmed from the fact that "Batjac, through its predecessor corporation Wayne-Fellows, made an oral agreement in May 1952 to pay Roos 2½% of its net profit before taxes ... On August 12, 1955 Fellows wrote Roos that he was suspending the arrangement as of July 31, 1954, more than a year earlier." The arbitrator noted that he was asked to decide "whether the Roos arrangement continued to the termination notice date, August 1955, or ceased as of July 31, 1954." He concluded that the termination occurred when the notice was given in 1955, not retroactively.

Meighan scolded:
"There is, however, a custom, and equity, in civilized business life to cushion the termination of an employment relationship ... Coincident with his last year or more, Roos, in addition to his normal duties involved in current and historical management matters was required to assume two additional responsibilities: (a) to educate Wayne's inside staff into the details of a very complex business pattern, and (b) to expend considerable initiative, energy and imagination to develop aspects of Wayne's future financial pattern."

Just how complicated their affairs were can be gleaned from the arbitrator's conclusions of September 1964:

Page	Issue	Decision
2	*Norwester*	"A purchase/sale proposal was formulated upon the mutual agreement of both parties the result of which was that Roos purchased the *Norwester*."
3	Sours Property, Acapulco	"Roos and Wayne own the Sours property equally. Expenses and capital contributions are to be made on an equal basis."
5	Graham-Michaelis Oil Lease	"The affairs of the venture were found to be in good order ... The undistributed balance due Wayne from Roos is to be paid Wayne ..."
6	Lancaster Property	"Wayne has traded his interest ... with Rex Allen for Allen's interest in the Los Flamingo's Hotel ... Wayne is now satisfied as to his complaint."
7	Polar Pantry, Inc.	"The entire circumstances ... were found to be equitable to all ..."
8	Westside Tennis Club	The club had been liquidated with oil rights reserved and leased to Signal Oil Co. The arbitrator wrote, "it was abundantly clear that the information sought (by Wayne) had been in the possession of Weesner, Wayne's financial man" for some time. Wayne had complained about the accounting, Dad's fees, etc. The arbitrator said Dad's fees for the liquidation, etc. were "reasonable."

9	Claim of Wayne to the Return of $8,800	Wayne claimed he had signed two checks "on the basis of inadequate or incorrect information ... Roos owes Wayne $8,800 in repayment of what is to be considered a loan."
10	Ione Ingle oil investment	"Wayne and Roos are equally involved. ... Roos owes Wayne $2,000 ..."
11	Insurance Service Bureau	"Agreement reached whereby Wayne's interest was acquired and grievances settled."
12	Beverly Wilshire Construction Co.	"Roos owes Wayne $16,438.66 plus interest for the note."
13-15	Arthur Andersen Fees	Wayne demanded that Roos share in the expense. Wayne withdrawn for 1957; Roos owes Wayne $4,375 for 1958 and 1959-60 fees were denied because their relationship had terminated.
16-18	Profits Due Roos From Fifth Corp., Wayne-Fellows Batjac	"Batjac owes Roos for services $27,632.71 for the year ending July 31, 1955, plus $52.41 for an underpayment for 1954."
19	Batjac Mexico & Batjac Panama	Roos claim denied.

20-26	Fees Due Roos as Business Manager	Due to Roos for:	
		Barbarian and the Geisha	$15,666.66
		Rio Bravo	$16,250
		Horse Soldiers	$35,000
		Total	$66,916.66

28	Culver Hotel	Final Decision when the hotel sale is completed.

In addition, the costs of the arbitrator ($10,000) and the accountants' fee for O'Melveny and Myers ($3,500) was split between Dad and Wayne.

Many issues were settled, and it seems to me where it was indicated money was owed from one to the other the net result was as follows:

Issue	Dad Owed Wayne	Wayne Owed Dad
Graham-Michaelis Oil Lease	Undist. Balance	
Return of $8,800 Note	$ 8,800	
Ione-Ingle Oil	$ 2,000	
Beverly-Wilshire Construction	$16,438.66 Note	
Arthur Andersen Fees	$ 4,375	
Profits due Roos from Fifth Corp., Wayne-Fellows or Batjac		$27,632.71 $52.41
Fees Due Roos as Business Manager		$66,916.66
Total:	**$31,613.66**	**$94,601.78**

It appears that the Wayne organizations owed a lot more money to Dad than he owed them.

Wayne's lawyers had complained that he was uninformed. Dad was scolded by the arbitrator because "his method of communicating to his client Wayne, and to his partner and business associate Wayne, lacked clarity, regularity, promptness or any uniform system. It is clear that a great part of the confusion as to Wayne's affairs and his general unhappiness with Roos stemmed from the inadequate method of communication used by Roos."

Our CPA, Al Marsella, sat in on the arbitration and said that Duke just glared at him a couple of times when he answered questions. Afterward, it had all blown over, and Duke came and put his arm around Al.

Ben Newman, Dad's attorney (and still mine), also sat in on the arbitration. He said Wayne's minions made it seem like a bullfight where they were the picadors, trying to impress Wayne, the matador, earning brownie points by poking barbs into the bull, my dad. Meanwhile, Ben told me Dad behaved like a gentleman and a class act, comporting himself with dignity. When it was over, Dad could have insisted on being paid the money due him. Instead, he was considerate and volunteered that Duke could spread the payment out.

One more comment needs to be made about the arbitrator's decision. He referred to Dad's putting together the Jim Wood cotton deal and concluded, "Wayne's inside staff wrestled it out of Roos' hands by December and took it over." When I asked my brother if he remembered that episode he said, "Hell, yes, I remember ... In fact I was there when Jim Wood, a brilliant young attorney, brought the deal to Dad. They put the whole thing together, gathered the investors, etc." Unfortunately, Dad and Jim didn't get the credit, or the profit.

Strangely, several people claim that Duke came up with the whole thing. That wasn't true. He didn't, "on his own ... buy several ranches in Arizona." Instead, the profitability of the ranches stemmed from the package Dad and Jim had put together. Initially the ranches were growing cotton, which wasn't making much money, until the government started subsidizing cotton farms to curtail their crops. Using those subsidies as capital, Duke and his then partners started raising cattle and feed instead. It's too bad Dad and Jim didn't get to see their plan succeed.

After Duke left Beverly Management Corporation, he turned over his business affairs to Don La Cava, who was married to his daughter Toni. Don handled his finances for three years until one day in 1965 Duke and Pilar had spent $20,000 to $30,000 in one weekend on a shopping spree. When the credit card bills came in, Don told them there was not enough money in the bank to cover them. La Cava was blamed for the problem and was replaced.

Liquid cash was a rarity in many Hollywood circles. It reminds me of the old story of a Hollywood producer planning a big blockbuster movie with top-notch stars. He promises they will all make a fortune until a lowly accountant points out, "To get started we need $10,000 cash" and the producer says, "Millions we'll make, but $10,000 cash—that kind of money we don't have!"

Duke's cash flow problems went on throughout his life. People continued to think of him as a soft touch for hard-luck stories, and he delivered both cash and sympathy. He had checkbooks all over the place and freely wrote checks without recording the amounts or who they were made out to.

His expenses were ongoing, with many family members on his payroll. Pilar and his second family were reportedly spending $200,000 a year. And he was in the top brackets as far as taxes were concerned. In 1977, two years before his death, he answered an invitation to appear at the Highland Gathering and Games in Long Beach with a letter to Marylin Hudson, saying he was *still* slaving for the IRS and banks.

Pilar Wayne wrote in her book *John Wayne—My Life with the Duke* that when Dad died, "his widow called Duke and begged him to attend the funeral. I was amazed at such a request, given all that had happened between the two men ..."

I was amazed at the story, too, because that isn't what happened. When Dad died, Mom didn't make the calls; *I* made all the calls. And if she had made the calls, she never would have begged; that was not in her nature. When I talked to Duke, I told him about Dad's death and asked him to be a pallbearer. He said, "Of course, honey. Tell me where to go and what to do." Differences aside, there were a lot of good memories and there was a last farewell.

When Duke died, his net worth was reportedly around $30 million, not a huge amount given his long and successful career. His money had supported three wives and seven children. He'd lived a good lifestyle for many years with yachts, houses, a private jet, and a helicopter. Enjoyed the company of many prominent people. Freely expressed his political views. Was a real American patriot. Traveled all over the world. Was admired by most and vilified by some. Won awards for his work. Had kids who loved him. Earned the respect of his fellow Americans. And, despite the obstacles, basically did what he wanted.

And had made movies he loved, among them *Stagecoach*, *They Were Expendable*, *Fort Apache*, *Rio Grande*, *The Quiet Man*, *Hatari*, *In Harm's Way*, *True Grit*, and the grand finale of his career, *The Shootist*, made three years before his death. In his book *Who The Hell's In It* Peter Bogdanovich recalls an interview with John Wayne on the set of *El Dorado* in 1965. After they talked for an hour, Duke said, "Jeez, it was good talkin' about—*pictures!* Christ, the only thing anybody ever talks to me about these days is—politics and cancer!"

The last time Mom, my brother, and I saw Duke was at the Big Canyon Country Club in Newport Beach, California. He came over and gave us a big hug and talked about the good old days. He shook hands with my brother and tapped his chest and said, "Dynie, watch your weight. Your Dad was a good example for you." Duke looked so thin, but he was as commanding a presence and as blustery as ever.

Despite any business problems, we were a mutual admiration society.

I remember the time when my youngest son, Jon, had read something about his grandfather in one of the books written about John Wayne. Jon telephoned Duke to say that he did not like what the authors had said about his granddad. Duke asked Jon to come over to talk about it. So Jon, sixteen at the time, got in his car and drove over from our house on Balboa Island to Duke's house in Bayshore. Duke actually apologized to Jon and told him, "I didn't say that. It was just something the publisher put in the book. I didn't endorse that book on my life."

Duke's eldest son, Michael, had been president of Batjac for some time and had produced many of his father's later films. I saw Michael at the Beverly Wilshire Hotel two or three weeks before he died. We hugged and reminisced a bit. It brought back a lot of memories.

There'll never be another John Wayne. We were proud to know him.

State of California

GOVERNOR'S OFFICE
SACRAMENTO

EARL WARREN
GOVERNOR

June 16, 1951

TO WHOM IT MAY CONCERN:

The bearer of this letter, Bo C.
Roos, is planning a trip to England and
Western Europe.

Mr. Roos is a resident of Beverly
Hills, California, a respected business
man, and a personal friend of many years.

I am sure that Mr. Roos will
reflect the friendly feeling which Californians
have for the people of the countries he will
visit, bound to us by the ties of history
and blood.

I shall appreciate any courtesies
extended to him in the course of his
travels.

Sincerely,

Governor

CHAPTER 9

It's Who You Know

A nytime you went in my Dad's office or my parents' home, you'd never know who'd be there. It could be clients, of course, but beyond that it might be a mayor or a prince; the chief of police; a top box office movie star, producer, or director; an up-and-coming nobody; visitors from South America, Europe, the Middle East, or the Orient; somebody's mistress; a couple on the verge of an affair, a wedding, or a divorce; family; or us kids and our friends.

Dad's transition from being a builder to being a Hollywood business manager came about when motion picture stars Bebe Daniels and her husband, Ben Lyon, came to him for financial advice in the early '30s. Ben was quoted as saying, "Bebe and I were Bö Roos's first star clients, and Bö lost no time in showing us what he could do. Bebe and I wanted a new apartment, but everywhere we were asked astronomical rents. 'Leave it to me,' said Bö, and he got a flat for us without revealing who he was acting for. We got it for 35 percent less than we had been asked in the first place." In appreciation they opened the doors to other people they knew in the industry.

At one time, Ben was the casting director at Twentieth Century Fox. Adela Rogers St. Johns claimed he "had a keen eye for talent, having discovered among others Jean Harlow and Marilyn Monroe." His part in making Marilyn Monroe a star has been debated, as has her iconic status as a "sex symbol." Sheilah Graham in *Hollywood Revisited* wrote that "while Marilyn went to bed with half of Hollywood, including Brando, Sinatra, and two members of the Kennedy family—JFK and Bobby—strangely she was a sex symbol who didn't care too much for sex." Go figure.

In 1935 Bebe and Ben moved to England after the Lindbergh baby kidnapping and a series of kidnap threats in Hollywood, which led many stars to hire guards for their children. Adela Rogers St. Johns, in her memoir of Hollywood *Love, Laughter, and Tears*, wrote, "an actual attempt was made to kidnap (their daughter) Barbara Bebe Lyon. District Attorney Buron Fitts advised her parents to leave the country until the insanity died down." Ben and Bebe built new careers in England and lived there for a good part of their married life. They were big stars through their BBC radio show and personal appearances entertaining the troops throughout World War II. They were often called "America's greatest good will ambassadors." The two always went out of their way to put out the welcome mat for Dad and anyone he'd send on to them, including my daughter Cathy who was treated royally when she and her husband went to London. Dad reciprocated generously, of course.

No one can debate that the business of Hollywood was fueled by discoveries. There have been various stories about Linda Christian and her relationship to my dad. Some people have said that Dad paid for Linda's education to become an actress and that she adopted his middle name, Christian, in honor of him. Others claim that he was instrumental in getting her a role in the film *Tarzan and the Mermaids* when his client Johnny Weissmuller told him they were looking for native talent to play in the film. Miguel Alemán was a good friend of Dad's, and it's often said that Dad suggested her for the part to Alemán or talked producer Sol Lesser into giving her the role. Whatever happened, Linda went on to a limited film career but a colorful personal life, including affairs with Errol Flynn and playboys "Baby" Pignatari and the Marquis de Portago, and married Tyrone Power and Edmund

Edward Bates from the Vatican with Mom and Dad in Rome.

Purdom. She wrote about her adventures in her memoir, *Linda*. As far as I can tell, my Dad is not mentioned.

Dad's network of contacts grew. He always had a friend or knew somebody who knew somebody, and was always on the lookout for putting people together and making things happen. His networking apparatus outside the film industry grew a lot through his activities with The Old Shoes Club, of which he was a director along with John Wayne, Red Skelton, and Ben Lyon. Columnist Frances Givens wrote in a Detroit paper about the only Detroit member, Ozzie Olson, president of Swedish Crucible Steel Co. and a director of the Detroit Lions football team, going back to Hollywood for a big reunion with the group at least once a year. The decorations for one party featured the club insignia— glistening yard-high shoes made of ice. The insignia was based on

Standing left to right: Dad with Club founder Oscar Olson, presdident of Swedish Crucible Steel Co. with Fred MacMurray. Seated are right to left: June Haver, Jeanie Olson, Mom ande two more friends.

Van Gogh's famous painting of *Old Shoes*. Members wore gold cufflinks with the shoe motif made for them at Ruser Jewelers on Rodeo Drive in Beverly Hills.

A note in my dad's files to Ozzie recalled that they had met in 1937 in Windsor, Canada, when Dad was traveling with Lupe Velez and Johnny Weissmuller for the opening of the water show in Cleveland, the first one he did, followed by shows in 1939, 1940, and the 1941 World's Fair. Later Dad wrote, "We then had a joint train trip when I was going to meet with Orson Welles and Cole Porter to make *Around the World in 80 Days*. You (and your wife) went with me to New York ... On that trip you met Orson Welles with me, but he was a crazy man, and I walked away from his production because he wouldn't protect himself. That was the original stage play." Orson Welles had been Dad's client, and when it came to his career, he had made some self-defeating moves.

The letter goes on to list various other members of The Old Shoes, including George Healy of the *Times-Picayune* newspaper, Ken Belieu, who had been an aide to the president for six years and was under secretary of the navy for President Kennedy, and Russ Stewart of the *Chicago Sun Times*. To get elected to membership a person had to be recommended by others, and Dad wrote, "some of the people I have sent to you (Ozzie) were Gene Raymond and Jeannette MacDonald about 1963 and Fred MacMurray, John Wayne, Ward Bond and oh, so many of them." (Ozzie, who owned a toilet seat manufacturing company, sent Dad a toilet seat sawed in half with the inscription "To my half-ass friend, Bö Roos.")

On a more dignified note, one of the members of The Old Shoes was Prince Bernhard of the Netherlands. Since his name (Prince Bernhard of Lippe-Biesterfeld) and his address (Soestdijk Palace, Soestdijk, Aaarn, the Netherlands) were impossible to spell, we all called him "P. B." He was married to Queen Juliana for more than six decades and was the father of Queen Beatrix. He had served as a pilot for the Allies in World War II and helped rebuild

Jeanie Olson with Old Shoes Member, actor Ward Bond, and Johnny Weissmuller

the Netherlands, which were devastated by Nazi occupation. He was known for having an "openly rocky marriage and affairs" and usually brought his girlfriend Lisa (Alicia) with him when he came to call. Mother loved Alicia, even with the infidelity. P. B. and Dad went on safari once in Africa, before Bernhard helped found the World Wildlife Fund in 1961, becoming its first chairman. When he died in 2004, the Associated Press said he was "tall, handsome and active into his 90s ... a dapper dresser who wore glasses and a trademark carnation in his lapel." Bernhard was a great friend of ours and loved to come over and cook with my dad, who was especially proud of his Swedish meatballs.

I remember when Beverly Hills was a small town, full of ambition and stress, but also full of fun. The fun sometimes required the police to straighten it out. The Beverly Hills Police

Department pretty much acted like a small-town police force, sorting out the big problems from the nuisances, and protecting its citizens from their own foolishness. For his part, Dad was a big booster of their efforts. Every time there was a fund-raiser or policemen's ball or benefit, or they needed somebody to stand up for them before the city council, Dad would be there. Key members of the force were invited to Dad's parties.

All the big stars had morals clauses in their contracts. If any indiscretions took place, the studios could drop their contract. It was to Dad's business benefit to have contacts among law enforcement agencies.

In return, many times a year the police would call Dad and help cover up a problem, whether it was being drunk and disorderly or in a fight of some kind. Dad would go right down to help if necessary, or the police would drive the star home first and call Dad afterward. He'd call his client's attorney, arrange for bail, calm down a belligerent spouse, plug any leaks to the press, reassure his "kids," help them get over the hangover the

Dad, with more of the Old Shoes members. Johnny Weissmuller, Rex Allen, Ozzie Olson and Red Skelton.

next morning, and counsel them on how to stay out of trouble the next time.

Dad got in trouble himself more than once—usually doing something that was called "madcap," crazy, or just goofy. Once he and Lupe Velez followed a night at the fights with an escapade in Beverly Hills. They had been talking about how Dad had delivered newspapers when he was a boy. She wanted to see how it was done, but there didn't seem to be any newspapers around, just the morning delivery of milk bottles. So the two of them proceeded to toss milk bottles on people's doorsteps with ear-shattering bangs until the cops showed up and sent them home with a stern warning. According to biographer Michael Freedland, once at the Mocambo when Errol Flynn had just slugged gossip columnist Jimmy Fidler, Lupe picked up a ketchup bottle and danced around Flynn, yelling, "Geeve eeet to heem, beeg boy."

Another time, Dad and his lawyer Frank Belcher, who was president of the bar association at the time, went to a party in Bel Air where they had a few drinks. When they started for home at 3 A.M., they decided to drive backward to their homes in Beverly Hills. After about a mile, an officer stopped them. He recognized them and asked what they were doing. Both of them looked at him innocently and said, "We are just going back to where we came from." The officer laughed with them and told them, "Not tonight. Turn it around and do it the right way, okay?" They're lucky they didn't get arrested and that the papers didn't pick up the story.

To illustrate how accommodating the police were, I remember another time when I was at Dad's Malibu house with others from the office going over the guest list for a party. Our next door neighbor, an airline pilot, knocked on the door and came in with two gorgeous "broads," as he called them, in tow. They breezed in and made themselves some drinks. Almost immediately the door opened again, and Dad and his chauffeur came in carrying a big basket of food. Dad said he heard we were working and decided to bring us a picnic. Dad always overbought everything, so we

Prince Bernhard of the Netherlands who was a jetsetting charismatic ambassador for his country. "PB" was co-founder of The World Wildlife Fund. He was consort to Queen Juliana and father of the present Queen Beatrix. He sent Christmas Cards each year with his greeting and entertained my Mom and Dad in his fantastic castle. They, in return, allowed him to cook in their kitchen during his many visits; a favorite pastime of his.

*A headline that would read: ARABIAN ROYAL
PRINCES HERE FOR CONFERENCE.*

*We entertained the Saudi Arabian Royalty with dinner at the famous
Ciro's restaurant, with dinner and dancing. The next day we took
them on a tour of Warner Brothers Studios. Pictured at the studio is
Sheik Ali Alireza, director Lew Borzage, me, and actor Pat O'Brien.
Pictured at dinner at Ciro's... Ali with his wife, Marianne, my Mom,
and my cousin Shirley Patton beside me. The visiting Prince is at the
head of the table with several Secret Service men also attending.*

AT AIRPORT—H.R.H. Amir Fahad Ibn Abdul Aziz, left; H.R.H. Amir Nawaf Ibn Abdul Aziz, center, both sons of King Ibn Saud of Saudi Arabia, and His Highness Amir Abdullah Al-Faisal after arrival from San Francisco.

had plenty of food when still another friend, Victor Mature, and his three Peruvian girlfriends joined us. The party took a different turn when one of the Peruvian women screamed and pointed to a rat that was running across the room. I jumped up on the couch, some girls were on top of the bar, and everybody was yelling when the rat ran into a closet. Dad quickly closed the closet door and called the Malibu Highway Patrol to "get the rat." Minutes later the cops arrived and found everyone still up on the furniture with drinks in their hands. One of the cops slowly opened the closet door and sprayed some kind of liquid into it, waited a moment, pulled his gun, and shot the rat "right between the eyes". Then he reached in, picked up the corpse, and tossed it into the ocean. All would have ended well, except that the bullet had gone through the thin closet wall and lodged in the water heater behind it, causing the water to gush out. Everybody collapsed laughing and had another drink!

Speaking of police, it was a good thing that the major studios had their own police departments. In fact, MGM Studios had a larger police force than that of Culver City, where MGM was located. In his book *Lion of Hollywood*, Scott Eyman quoted MGM head of publicity Howard Strickling describing how they handled "the multiple-problem ... violent alcoholic [Spencer Tracy]" by keeping "an official-looking ambulance on call at the studio" that was recognized by bar owners and hotel managers who "knew what to do if Tracy showed up drunk and began causing a problem." They would call Strickling, who would call the MGM police chief, who would dispatch a couple of men disguised as paramedics to "rescue" Tracy. Tracy wasn't one of our clients, thank goodness.

We enjoyed and entertained many prominent people who were our guests when they came to town. One of them was Ali Alireza, whom Dad had met at Scripps Clinic in La Jolla when Ali was still a student at Berkeley. In 1938 Dad had had a liver ailment diagnosed and was given two years to live. He was sure the treatment at Scripps had saved his life and kept going back for an annual checkup.

When Ali came to Hollywood, he called on Dad, and I have a picture of several of us with him at the Mocambo. Columnist Florabel Muir reported on our guests as "a couple of dyed-in-the-burnoose sheiks of Araby, real big shots from the realm of King Ibn Saud." She further reported that "these sheiks were Mohammed Ali Reza and a cousin Ahmed Ali Reza and they had told her that they do not spend their time coursing over the hot desert sands in pursuit of maidens swooning for love of them, but rather they

A papal audience and blessing for young Richard Skelton who was suffering from leukemia. An audience arranged by my father and including Red and his wife, Georgia along with daughter Valentina.

ride around in Cadillacs and deal in top-dollar diplomacy ... and that they are entrusted with the control of vast enterprises. Ibn Saud has acquired a fleet of tankers to convey his huge oil reserves to the rest of the world. Unquote." (The last I heard in April 2005 President Bush was meeting with Saudi Crown Prince Abdullah, and the oil pumping capacity of Saudi Arabia was around 10 million barrels a day! Really "vast enterprises.")

Once when there was the threat of a cholera epidemic in Saudi Arabia and the government couldn't obtain a supply of the rare anticholera serum, Ali, who later became a minister plenipotentiary of Saudi Arabia, called Dad from Paris for help. Dad pulled some strings, and within seventy-two hours 200,000 units of anticholera serum were being dispensed in Saudi Arabia. For years, Dad wore the beautiful gold watch the Saudi king had sent him with his thanks engraved on the back. (My brother has the watch now.)

Ali married an American, Marianne St. John, whom he had met at the university. She and I still keep in touch. I love to hear her describe the primitive conditions and social strictures that awaited her when she arrived in Saudi Arabia and what it was like to get transformed from a typical American college girl into an Arabian woman wearing a chador and living in a harem with the rest of the womenfolk. Marianne wrote about the experience in her memoir, *At the Drop of a Veil*.

Dad's contacts were really tapped when Red Skelton's young son Richard developed leukemia. Red wanted to take him for a trip around the world and put his performing schedule on hold. Dad helped to arrange the trip for Red and his family, starting at the Hotel Los Flamingos in Mexico. He also arranged a papal audience and accompanied the family to the Vatican. Afterward the Skeltons traveled all over Europe, the Middle East, and the Orient and finally arrived in Hawaii, where Richard relapsed and was put in the hospital. My dad's secretary at the time was David Armstrong's mother. David, a high school student, worked in the office during the summer. He wrote us a note describing what it was like when Red called our office from Hawaii: "The call was put on the intercom throughout the office. Richard had asked his father to do the 'Guzzlers Gin' skit for him. Red was going through the routine when suddenly he stopped, and one just heard silence. Then Red said, 'Goodbye, Richard. God bless.' Everyone at Beverly Management was crying, but you know, Red returned, put on his wonderful smile and again became 'America's Clown.'" Some people claimed it was all a publicity stunt, as if losing a child wouldn't be a heartbreaker. They say every clown is touched in sadness. We knew that firsthand.

Red Skelton and Dad in a hot Gin Rummy Game.

CHAPTER 10

RED SKELTON

Red used to say, "I'm nuts, and I know it." I can attest to the fact that he drove a lot of us close to him a little nuts, too! He believed that God put everyone on the earth for some purpose, and that his was to make people laugh. He thought of himself as a clown, as was his father, who died two months before Red was born. P. T. Barnum once said, "Clowns are pegs used to hang circuses on." Red used his clowning as a peg to hang more than one entertainment medium on, not just circuses. From a debut on a medicine show at the age of ten, he clowned his way through tent shows, minstrels, circuses, burlesques, Mississippi showboats, vaudeville, radio, movies, nightclubs, the stage, and TV. Did I mention personal appearances? According to Elsie Hix, after Red enlisted in the army as a private in World War II, he was assigned to entertaining the troops, and during a two-year period he gave 3,800 shows on troop carrier hospital ships. It was amazing how he adapted to every medium and made a success of it. But that didn't explain the rest of him. Talented guy. Charming guy. Strange guy.

Skelton was one of our biggest clients and one of our most complicated and challenging accounts. He was a lot of fun, but he was truly hard to handle, and his professional, business, personal, and romantic lives were even more complicated than most.

145

As his business managers we had a lot to contend with, and it all came together like a wide-screen soap opera on a trip we took together to New York in the early '40s. Our entourage consisted of Red himself, two of his press agents, his valet, his wife, Edna, his girlfriend Muriel, Dad, and me. It was not going to be an easy trip. It started calmly as the *Super Chief* pulled away from Union Station in Los Angeles, stopping at the Glendale Railroad Station twenty minutes later to pick up a few passengers. Many actors and actresses preferred to board the train in Glendale or Pasadena to avoid the news reporters who kept an eye on arrivals and departures at the main station. The stars loved publicity when it made them look good, hated it when they had something to hide.

Dad and I settled into our individual compartments for a rest, and then I went to join him in the club car. I got a few wolf whistles on the way from some guys in uniform, smiled back, and got salutes in return. It's probably not politically correct nowadays, but I was a girly girl and enjoyed the attention. Still do!

Red, Dad and well-known author Gene Fowler attending a banquet in London.

*Red Skelton, Dad and I at the top of the Empire State Building with
Milton Weiss and a friend. during our trip to New York in 1942.*

I found Dad in the club car with Red and Red's girlfriend Muriel.
(Edna had a headache, so she had stayed in her compartment.)
Red was doing one of his favorite stage routines "pantomiming"
threading a needle and sewing a button on his jacket and keeping
his fellow passengers entertained. He loved making people laugh,
and they loved him for it.

While Red was clowning, Dad and I spent a lot of time going
over the agenda for the two weeks of business meetings we had
scheduled in New York, including meetings with Herbert Yates,
president of Republic Studios.

Throughout everything, we were especially sensitive to any
negative publicity. Red's shows were family oriented, and the

Dad at far left, with Freeman Keyes on the right...
celebrating young Richard Skelton's birthday.

networks and sponsors took a dim view of adverse publicity surrounding their actors and actresses. It would not be easy keeping his romantic life out of the papers. When we got to New York, Dad tended to business while I took the girlfriend out on a shopping spree, knowing that Edna was back at the hotel, ushering in another girl whom Red had met the day before. I had to call Edna before bringing Muriel back to the hotel, so that she could get the latest girl out of our star's suite before the current girlfriend walked in. Talk about an awkward situation. I also had to keep an eye on Red's "disappearing act." At the time

SAVOY HOTEL LONDON

TELEPHONE, TEMPLE BAR 4343   TELEGRAMS, SAVOTEL LONDON

*Red's handwriting demands a translation, but I've kept his colorful spelling:
To Freeman Keyes at Pamlowe Guild, Chicago. "Sorry you can't join us...
things are really fun here. Now about of TV. Beings we are going live I see
no reason to rush back but would segest that writers have scrip redy as I can't
not afford under the one clause in the contract allow 28 years of materials
to become property of Russell M. Seeds. In radio that clause was of no
importance, but if any of the skits that I have are o be used in TV I must
have in writing from them that they revert back to me as sole owner. We may
go back to Rome from here for a few days... then to France. Sorry you can't
join us. Will write you soon. Best to all, Always Red Skelton." Note: This
would have been written around 1950 and illustrates the changing issues
in creative property rights as our clients moved from one medium to another.
"Snail mail" was the way of communication in those days, or in person.*

1952 Awards Banquet of the Academy of Television Arts & Sciences held at the Coconut Grove where Red won the Emmy for best comedy show in 1951. At their table with Red and Georgia were Mom and Dad, along with Red's publicity man, Milton Weiss, and his wife Edith.

4th Annual Awards Dinner
Academy of Television Arts & Sciences
Ambassador Hotel- Los Angeles, Calif.
February 18, 1952

he didn't drink or smoke. When he escaped his complicated life, it was usually to go somewhere isolated to paint. I had to track him down more than once. Once he and I boarded a subway, and the conductor took us both to the large bubble in front where we could watch the engineer run the train. A wild ride to say the least. Red and Edna had married in 1931 when he was seventeen and she was sixteen. She was a theater usher at the time, and he was a comic on stage. Times were lean, and when they needed money, she would enter a walkathon, and he would be the master of ceremonies. According to Arthur Marx's biography of Red, *Red Skelton*, a chapter of which was excerpted in *The Enquirer*, in one marathon, "She had danced 2½ consecutive months (with a 10 minute 'break' every hour) and won the $500 first prize—only to have it stolen from her when she fell into a coma-like sleep in a dressing room after the contest." In her later years, Edna paid a bitter price for the abuse her feet and legs were subjected to, becoming crippled and barely able to walk.

Jobs for comics were few, audiences were tough and broke, and to get laughs the stunts got more bizarre. Trying to loosen up an audience at one engagement, Red borrowed a kid's bicycle and drove it around the parapet on the balcony. It got laughs when he fell down fifteen feet, but in the process he broke two ribs and an arm. Through it all, Edna was not only his wife, but his buddy and mother figure. She wrote many of his comedy routines and later was producer of his television show. She even became his agent, negotiating for him a $5 million, seven-year Hollywood contract in 1951, so we had a lot of dealings with her. The two of them carried a lot of history together. She loved him and catered to his whims, such as answering all his phone calls because he hated to talk on the phone. He called her Mom and admitted that he was her "bad little boy." When it came to his other women, she was forgiving of her "bad little boy".

The next girlfriend was a beautiful young redhead, Georgia Davis, who confronted Edna and told her flat out that she was going to take Red away from her permanently, marry him, and then have two children right away so she would be set up financially for life. Edna couldn't have children; Red wanted them. Edna tried to tell Red about Georgia's threat, but he would not believe it. She told us, too, and Dad and I could barely believe it ourselves, but we soon saw how Georgia was getting a firm foothold in Red's life. We were afraid he was on the brink of leaving Edna without having thought it through. Of course, he refused to discuss it. All we needed was headlines that read: "Clown Dumps Devoted Wife for Young Beauty." Our worries didn't help. Eventually he and Edna divorced, and he and Georgia got married and did have the two children. Dad was godfather to their daughter, Valentina.

I liked Edna very much, and she continued to work with Red for years after, but maybe she didn't fulfill all his personal needs. When she divorced him, she was quoted in the London *Daily Mirror* as saying, "I just can't stand living with a mental twelve-year old."

After Red and Georgia were married, Dad told me that someone in our office had received a call from one of the columnists inquiring about the story that she had heard that Red and Georgia had ordered two girls from an agency to spend the night with them. He had lied to the columnist that it was just someone's wild imagination, but it did remind him of some of the stories he had heard about their masseur, who had been living with them for a few weeks during the summer. Georgia and Red sometimes were like a couple of bad little kids, playing with adult emotions. I just hoped the children were being sheltered from the antics.

Both Red and Georgia liked to spend money. They had a house in Bel Air and a place in the desert, and, of course, both houses were filled with every toy imaginable—for the adults and the kids. The columnist Jim Bacon wrote in *Hollywood Is a Four Letter Town*, "Once Red invited me to drop by his house in Palm Springs for a drink. I drove past and saw eight Rolls Royces in the driveway; I thought he was having a party, so I didn't go in. But I found out—they all belonged to him." I remember they were all in different colors.

Edna had tried to keep Red's spending in check, but keeping track of his money was a huge challenge for all of us. He'd been so poor as a child, he started carrying around thousands of dollars in cash or traveler's checks just to give him a feeling of security. Once he took $17,000 in cash, the proceeds from a show, onto an airplane, forgot about it, and never got it back. He spent like crazy, ordering twenty-five suits at one time and having a closet full of 200 neckties, all in the same color. Edna had let him have a bank account, but with the provision that he write on the check stub exactly what the check was written for so she could keep track of his expenses. His notations on the check stubs didn't help her (or our) accounting. He had written things like "For darned foolishness," "for rotten food," "really wasted," and "none of your business."

As his business manager, Dad gave him a weekly allowance, which led to more than one fight when Red demanded more money. Once Dad got a call from the police telling him to come to Hollywood and Vine because Skelton was causing a traffic jam. When Dad got there, Skelton was sitting in a director's chair in the middle of the intersection with signs around him reading

DOWN WITH BUSINESS MANAGERS
I WANT MORE SPENDING MONEY
75 cents for a tour of movie stars' homes
conducted by yours truly

Some tourists did take Red up on his offer and got in his limo for a ride around the block. Dad posed for a picture with Red, taken by the photographer Red brought with him, and told Red, "Okay, you win, but if you end up broke, don't blame me."

To show you how crazy Red could be, one night Dad got a call in the middle of the night. It was Georgia crying, "Oh, Bo, I've killed him, I've killed him." Dad jumped out of bed, put his pants on over his pajamas, and raced over to the Skelton home, where he found the front door open. He went in and found Georgia sitting on a chair crying, and Red stretched out on the floor with a knife protruding from his chest and blood all over the place. Dad was very suspicious and said, "You son of a bitch, you got me out of bed. Get up!" Of course, Red started laughing and stood up. Red needed only three to four hours of sleep a night and often used that time to get into mischief and probably do a lot of his clown paintings.

I remember another trip to New York with Red in the late 1940s that was more focused on business with a lot of deals in the works. There was the movie he was to star in for MGM, contracts for personal appearances, and details of the upcoming television show. The appointments were all set up, and the only problem would be to keep Red in our sights as much as possible.

Most of our attention was focused on the TV show, a new medium that affected all the other facets of show business. In 1946 there had been only 10,000 TV sets in the United States, according to *A Pictorial History of Television*. By 1951 the number had jumped to 12 million sets. It was amazing how fast the medium grew. The networks were scrambling to produce enough material to keep viewers coming. That era is often called the Golden Age of Comedy, and one after another the comedy greats turned to TV—Milton Berle, Sid Caesar, Groucho Marx, Ken Murray, Eddie Cantor, Jack Benny, Danny Thomas, Phil Silvers, and many more.

Red was worried about a lot of things. He wouldn't agree to one clause in the contract that would "allow 28 years of material to become the property of Russell M. Seeds," the show's producer. Red wrote, "If any of the skits that I have are to be used in TV I must have it in writing that they revert back to me as soul (sic) owner." (Red's spelling was not too great.)

Red was known for keeping his writers in turmoil. Writer Mel Diamond, who I don't think ever worked for Red, described the people writing for television this way: "Most of us came from radio. We thought TV was radio with pictures, so we wrote just the way we had done all along."

It's interesting how the demands on performers changed. In vaudeville and on the stage they worked in a visual and audio medium. Silent films were pictures only, except for the tinkly pianos in the theaters. When talkies came in, actors had to have voices. Those who failed a voice test were dropped, and those who passed were hailed with shouts of, "He can talk!" That brought a lot of stage performers to Hollywood since they could act *and* talk. Radio required just sound, but isn't it strange how when people listened to the radio in the "old" days, they congregated around the radio and looked at it as if they could see something inside? With television, they were back to a visual and audio medium. Red knew a visual medium required major adjustments in the writing, and changed his comedy arsenal to fit the small screen. He also insisted that NBC build him just exactly the kind of studio he wanted. He also wanted his shows taped, but he and Dad couldn't get the unions to agree. As a result, initially all the shows had to be done live, causing much more work and stress. It also meant that the early shows wouldn't be preserved for future audiences. In movies you could retake scenes over and over until the director was satisfied. With television you did it once, good or bad. Even when shows began to be filmed, their budgets didn't allow for extensive retakes.

Another thing performers worried about was audience reaction. The television studios were small and accommodated few people. If they didn't laugh, you were in trouble. That problem was solved with the invention of the "laugh machine," where you prerecorded a laugh track and pushed buttons to ensure that the jokes got a laugh. I understand that many of the laughs that were recorded on the master tapes came from Red Skelton shows.

At one point, there was so much TV work that NBC hired Dad to spend extra time with Red to keep things going smoothly. In fact, Dad and David Rose (who was Red's musical conductor) and his wife, Betty, appeared in a Christmas television program on Red's show.

Red's show debuted in 1951 and went on for twenty years. The show was on NBC from 1951 to 1953, then moved to CBS from 1953 to 1970, and returned to NBC from 1970 to 1971. In 1951 Red won the Emmy for Best Comedian or Comedienne "over a powerhouse list of nominees that included not only (Sid) Caesar and (Imogene) Coca but Lucille Ball, Jimmy Durante, and the popular team of Dean Martin and Jerry Lewis," according to *The Best of Television*, a chronicle of fifty years of Emmys. Red received the Governor's Award in 1986 and in 1988 was inducted into the TV Academy Hall of Fame.

While working on his upcoming television show, we were also preparing for Red's upcoming appearance at the London Palladium. Dad went with him to London for the show and called me from the Savoy to tell me Red had knocked them dead! There were thirty-nine long stretches of applause. The newspapers said Red had "captured the London audience in a way rarely equaled in the Palladium's history."

An interesting aside to Red's career was included in the *New York Times* obituary for Johnny Carson, which said Red showed up unannounced on *Carson's Cellar* show on KNXT in Los Angeles, which was later canceled. However, "Mr. Skelton thought so highly of Mr. Carson's work that he hired him as a writer of his own CBS television show." In 1954 Red was injured while doing a stunt, and CBS called on Carson to substitute for him. Impressed by his work, CBS offered Johnny his own show.

What a lot of talent Red had! According to *Celebrity Register*, Red was "a prolific writer and composer (4,000 short stories, 5,000 musical selections, 64 symphonies)," and movies from 1938 to the early 1950s, and "he has scripted his own radio, television, and personal appearance programs." When his television show was canceled, he told a Las Vegas audience that his heart was broken. In 1984 he started another new career—selling videocassettes of his television programs, which are still offered for sale. His paintings were snapped up by collectors.

*Bo, Sr. and Bo, Jr. having a discussion in front of the painting
done by Red Skelton, depicting Dad as a Clown.*

The cassettes and DVDs feature some of his best-known routines in the roles of Clem Kadiddlehopper, The Mean Widdle Kid, drunk Willie Lump-Lump, and Hobo Freddie the Freeloader. He'll be remembered for creating those characters by generations to come.

He also lives on in his clown paintings, which incorporate the sadness of clowns as well as their eagerness to make people laugh. I have two of Red's originals looking down on me from my living room wall. Red once painted our dad as a clown. My brother has the original painting in his home.

My husband, Ted, and I ran into Red in a department store in San Francisco a week or two before he married his third wife. We had a fun-filled reunion and wished the two of them much happiness. The last time I saw Red was when he visited with me in my office in Disneyland, and we rode the Monsanto Adventure Ride Through Inner Space together. He was his same sweet self.

Red died at the age of eighty-four in 1997. As I said at the beginning—talented guy, charming guy, sweet guy. As both Red and Dad often said, "God bless."

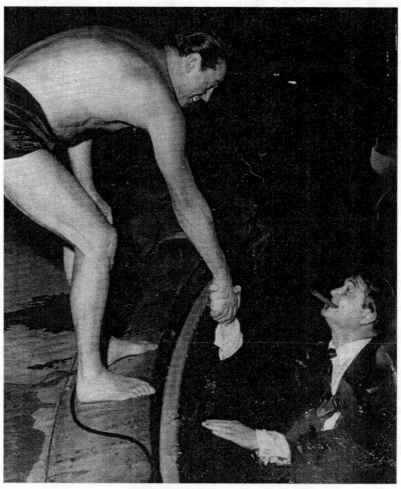

Clowning as usual, Red jumped into our pool during a party and Johnny Weissmuller helped pull him out

CHAPTER 11
"Nitty Gritty $$$"

The entertainment industry changed drastically after BMC began business in 1932. At that time there was no television, there were no home videos, and there was not much product licensing. The business was run basically by the studios and their moguls who controlled everything from scripts to casting, distribution to publicity, deal making to contracts, even how the stars lived their personal lives. Today the business is dominated by huge conglomerates with a wide range of control over many media—films, TV, publishing, recordings, tapes, cable, and so on. Many more stars own their own production companies and control what they film and how they capitalize on their names. (I wonder how Humphrey Bogart would have felt about the Bogart line of furniture we see advertised on TV! And I could just see John Wayne reacting to a cork with his likeness on top of a bourbon bottle!) Back then, Alfred Hitchcock said actors should be treated like "furniture." If so, it's pretty expensive furniture! Just as an example Arnold Schwarzenegger got $29.5 million for making *Terminator 3*. He also was to receive 20 percent of gross receipts from worldwide revenue and perks.

In the years we were in business we were part of many of those changes firsthand. Beverly Management Corporation's investments spanned a wide range of activities and were worldwide. It was a challenge and an exciting one. Dad looked at every situation from

Directors OF THE
CALIFORNIA CABAÑA CLUB

Frank Borzage   John Wayne   Johnny Weissmuller   Bo C. Roos   Red Skelton

George Brent   Joan Crawford   Ann Dvorak   Leslie Fenton   E. O. (Neil) Gurney

Fred MacMurray   Merle Oberon   Harriet Parsons   George Seaton   Edna Skelton Borzage   Robert Walker

THE BOARD OF DIRECTORS OF THE CABANA CLUB

The Cabana Club was billed as "a new conception in the historic trend of exclusive social clubs in Western America... with provisions for name bands, superb entertainment and a combined social and recreational program on a scale of grandeur never before attempted by any similar club. The California Cabana Club is especially fortunate in the personnel of both owners and board of directors, including as it does, some of the many outstanding stars of radio, stage and screen, together with business leaders whose records and personality are alike outstanding in the business of civic life of Southern California.

a moneyman's point of view. The litmus test was whether it could make money.

Investments involve risk, and not every venture was successful. The *New York Times* quoted Dad as saying, "I've been called a gambler for one reason—I'm only good for the client who wants action for his money. A lot of business managers never stick their necks out, and so they're never wrong. But I know my kids have only so long to get well in, so somebody has to carry the ball."

Carrying the ball got complicated, as illustrated by this typical meeting agenda:

Beverly Management Corporation
400 North Camden Drive
Beverly Hills, California
Crestview 1-5611

TO: Memo to Staff
FROM: Bö Chr. Roos, Sr.

SUBJECT: Requirements for Meeting

REQUIREMENTS | ANSWERS—AS BEST I REMEMBER

1. and 2. Income Projection— Cash Flow

I want the figures presented to us — the correct figures as we know them today. I want the total amount of capital dollars that went out in 1957 and 1958. I don't care where they came from. Just outgoing capital dollars—not incoming.

3. Information on Existing Investments

a) Venezuelan Partnership

I want everything we have... (including) ... the letters between McGrath-Arias-Wayne partnership. I want a statement of the total gross dollars we have sent to each of the partnerships—Arias, Ocean Products, Shrimp Boats, etc. In the other column, Venezuela, Oil Deal. Third column Venezuela lots. We want to be supplied with the situation on Batjac, Panama—Batjac, Mexico—and any other known company outside the U.S.A. connected with John Wayne, or his companies, or corporation stock.

Some of Dad's financial relationships with John Wayne are covered in detail elsewhere.

b) Polar Pantry

I want a Photostat of the letter handed to me today by Mr. Patric Knowles.

Polar Pantry was put together during World War II because it was not easy to get meat. Dad and Rex Allen, Frank Borzage, Patric Knowles, Fred MacMurray, and Lloyd Nolan backed it. Freezer lockers were rented on a monthly basis. Some of the meat came from MacMurray's ranch. Initially profitable, freezer lockers became obsolete when refrigerators were built with freezer compartments.

Dad and Fred MacMurray discussing... what else? Ways to make money. Here they are in front of the Polar Pantry, a frozen food locker company that many of the BMC clients sponsored during WWII. Fred was considered to be one of the richest actors to come out of Hollywood and made Dad proud. Fred and his wife June Haver were clients during most of the years that Dad operated the Beverly Management Corporation.

c) Culver Hotel

Mr. Kivel will have all the figures.
Get any figures we have, also the
Continental papers that were sent to
Belcher and returned to us.

My brother recalls it as the
Flatiron Building. The hotel,
built in 1924, is listed on
its Web site as an "elegant
boutique hotel awarded
'Landmark' status by Culver
City,and is listed on the
National Register of Historic
Places." In her memoir, Pilar
Wayne said the hotel operated
in the red for years and was
given to the YMCA by Duke,
"after he fired Roos." It was
a bit more complicated than
that. The *Westside Weekly*
newspaper reported, "At one
time, John Wayne was the
proprietor, reportedly winning
it in a poker bet." Although
the hotel operated as a hotel,
ownership kept bouncing from
one BMC client to another
for tax purposes. It was once
the part-time residence of
Ronald Reagan, and Duke,
Dad, and Red kept suites there.
The Munchkins stayed there
during the filming of the 1939
blockbuster *The Wizard of Oz*.
More recently, the hotel served
as a backdrop for the 1993
movie thriller *Last Action Hero*,
with Arnold Schwarzenegger.

d) Beverly Wilshire
   Construction Company

Financial statement showing profit
(stock profit at the moment)

Architect/Builder Kenneth
Albright owned the company
jointly with Dad.

e) Wayne Snow Oil

I want a statement showing everything paid out to date. Also, if it is correct—or do we owe.

f) Los Flamingos Hotel

Can't answer until we get the Arthur Andersen statement.

The Los Flamingos was a hubbub of business and social activity for Dad and his clients. Its story is told in detail elsewhere.

g) Fruehauf Stock

Would like information and dates on *all* Mr. Wayne's stock list.

h) Miscellaneous Oil Deals

Dick Igol, B & R, Graham-Michaells, Belcher & Roos. Tiger Minerals, Doug Johnson, the one in Nebraska, etc. I want the status of all the companies. We have letter to prove up Tiger Minerals. Also a statement on suggestions from Bill Green on what to do with B & R.

B & R Oil was named for Belcher & Roos. Fred MacMurray took tax write-offs for various deals over the years. Incidentally, whenever property was sold, Dad insisted that the oil and mineral rights be retained unless it enhanced the sale to have them included.

i) Mr. Rumple

This should be Mr. Rumple *and* Top Banana. How much put in and how much we have gotten out. Take information from the last letters explaining London financing.

Top Banana was a stage show starring Phil Silvers (Sgt. Bilko)and was filmed at the New York Winter Garden.

j) Panama (Tito)

That's a story in itself and is covered later in this chapter.

k) Rowley and Associates

Hold in abeyance.

Rowley ran BMC Insurance Service Bureau. It was later sold to Bob Thom.

l) Markets

m) Berkeley Books

We want to know when the $50,000 was put up. This should be on one of the memos of the meetings which Miss St. John sends out. The $50,000 was paid to Berkeley. How much have we received from Berkeley?

St. John was John Wayne's secretary.

n) Christian's Hut

Will review this verbally.

This landmark originated on Catalina at the Isthmus, now Two Harbors. It was a popular bar and restaurant and provided sleeping quarters for Clark Gable when he played Fletcher Christian in *Mutiny on the Bounty.* When Art La Shelle left the employ of William Wrigley, he opened Christian's Hut on the peninsula at Balboa, just down from the ferry. The sand-floored ground-level bar and Tahitian restaurant upstairs were favorites of Humphrey Bogart, Howard Hughes, Red Skelton, and other stars. Dad and John Wayne had some money in it. The three of them also owned several apartments in the area, as did Edna Skelton. Patric Knowles set up some Pedalos out in front where you could rent a boat and cruise the harbor.

o) The Boat

We leased it here in the office for a group from Texas from August 8th to the 22nd. It is leased from Aug. to Sept. 12. If he reduced the rates slightly, it would be about $1,000–$3,300 a day. The Skipper is paid separately by the people.

This was Dad's yacht, the 45-foot *Amaroo II,* which was periodically chartered. I remember Eugene Dukette was the skipper.

4. OTHER PERTINENT MATTERS

<u>a) The 1954, 1955 Income Taxes</u>

We will discuss the 1952 and 1953
settlement returns at the same time.

<u>b) Status of 30% withhold of E. Wayne</u>
E. Wayne was Duke's second
wife, Esperanza.

<u>c) Louise Avenue Insurance Settlement</u>

George has checks. Photostat copies
should be made.

<u>d) Warner Brothers</u>

<u>e) Josephine Wayne Settlement</u>

This should come from Art Roos. Copy
of projection given to BCR by Mr.
Weesner (of Arthur Andersen)—to be
used in the proposals for a settlement
with Mrs. Wayne.

See Chapter 7 for details of
Duke's divorces.

Most investments carried a risk with them, and Dad made
sure everyone involved knew that. I think our batting average
was extremely good, but there was one deal that bothered my dad
more than any other.

The *Los Angeles Times* on May 24, 1946, reported: "Details
of the pending purchase of the Santa Monica Deauville Club
from the L.A. Athletic Club by motion picture stars and other
stockholders of the Beverly Management Corporation to establish
an exclusive Beach Club at Santa Monica were disclosed yesterday.
The new club, to be known as the Cabana Club ... will embody
an outside pool with surrounding Cabanas, Bö Roos, head of

Beverly Management, said. Film colony figures taking part in the purchase ... include Joan Crawford, George Brent, Robert Walker, Frank Borzage, Red Skelton, Edna Skelton, John Wayne, Fred MacMurray, Leslie Fenton, George Seaton, Ann Dvorak, and Harriet Parsons. It was reported that the sale price is around 275 thousand dollars."

As the club prospectus stated, we thought the club "would directly contribute to the enhancement of community life in Southern California." The article went on to describe it as a streamlined, chromium, glass, and steel beach club, "which was promoted with a fortune spent on advertising and elaborate publicity parties. It didn't click. Although membership fees were high, the club was not exclusive enough to be smart. Because it

Dad and Edna Skelton looking at a rendering of the proposed CALIFORNIA COUNTRY CLUB, which became a successful golf club where my Dad and my brother and so many clients often played.

My brother, Bö, above and on the far right...
Bringing a bit of levity to the fact that someone had
removed some files from our safe the night before.

wasn't smart, it flopped ... Bö Roos admits that he and his clients gambled wrongly on that occasion."

Richard English wrote an extensive article about the situation in the *Saturday Evening Post* in February 1951:

"For all his success, Roos has a sore spot the size of the Empire State Building. On August 13, 1947 the Cabana Club, a modernistic Santa Monica beach club backed by a Roos syndicate of clients, failed to the tune of $901,874.28 ... the club was a failure from the start ...

"Hollywood's gossip soon began taking Roos apart at the seams. While other business managers modestly pointed out to their clients how safe their Government bonds were, Bö's 'kids' went for a ride." Dad was among the ones losing money. He dropped about $75,000 before it was over. A few of his clients stayed on with him until the whole thing was settled.

Some clients were bitter and left BMC, including Joan Crawford, Merle Oberon, and George Brent. Supposedly, the Hollywood trade papers ran editorials demanding an investigation of the business of business managers. There must have been some editorials. I had someone check the trade papers on file at the Academy of Motion Picture Arts & Sciences Library, but they couldn't find them.

Dad was feisty about the whole thing. He was quoted as saying that some of his fellow business managers were "guys going through life with nothing on their chest." (Shades of Governor Arnold Schwarzenegger calling some people "girly men"!) The business managers responded, and Richard English quoted one of them as saying, "We think a promoter functioning as a business manager is damaging to us all. Roos uses too spectacular means of putting his clients on a sound basis. And, as a participant in his own deals, he can't have the perspective a real business manager should maintain."

Not everyone criticized Dad's business philosophy of mixing his clients' money with his own. Some considered it a very sound practice. In 2006 Christopher Knight reported in the *Los Angeles*

Times about corporate problems and "our foul era of Enron, Tyco, World-com, Adelphia, Exon Mobil and the rest." He called it a problem stemming from "other people's money," quoting economist Adam Smith's *The Wealth of Nations* published in 1776. Smith wrote that, "managers ... using other people's money rather than their own" led to "negligence and ... extravagance" since managers were "not likely to exercise the same anxious vigilance with which the partners in a private guild frequently watch over their own." Dad didn't have a problem with being "absolutely vigilant," because his money was right in the pool alongside his clients'.

The Hollywood Reporter reported on August 14, 1947:

"Calif. Cabana Club Folding Tomorrow"

"The California Cabana Club in Santa Monica, will close its doors tomorrow and file a voluntary petition of bankruptcy. Although the club apparently could not operate profitably, it was learned yesterday that there are plenty of assets and 'very few' liabilities outside of the original investors. No trade creditors or employees will suffer any financial losses. Most of the backers are in the high brackets and are said to be taking their losses stoically. The principal regret is that one of the most beautiful clubs in America could not get the support of the community and that the anticipated membership did not materialize. The original initial fee was $800 when the club opened in April, 1946, and the lowering of the fee to $200 did not help substantially. The consensus is that the club was 10 years ahead of its time."

I agree; the timing was wrong. Previously, BMC had invested with its clients in a couple of country clubs, including the Westside Tennis Club and the California Country Club, which was a golf club. (See Chapter 12 for details.) It was not farfetched to expect that a beach club could work. Unfortunately, it didn't turn out that way. It was a big disappointment.

One of the items on the meeting agenda was Tito (Panama). Dad knew many people in the world, including the Arias family of Panama, who had played important roles in their country's politics for generations. Dad had introduced John Wayne to them, and they were all friends for many years. When Tito was courting the legendary prima ballerina Margo Fonteyn, she was dancing in Los Angeles once, and John Wayne lent them his yacht to take a group of dancers on an excursion to Catalina. The press covered every move of the glamorous dancer and the Panamanian jet setter diplomat. When they married in Paris in 1955, there were so many press photographers, they made a deafening racket, making it hard to hear the marriage vows.

Tito was appointed the Panamanian ambassador to England. In her autobiography Fonteyn wrote that when John Wayne visited London, they gave a large party for him and his entourage, including Bö Roos, "a man of outsize personality and zest." As the guests were leaving, one was about to take a hat he thought was his, but when he looked inside, there was this inscription: "To hell it's yours, put it back!" She wrote that the hat, Bö Roos, and three of the guests were still there the next morning as she was leaving for ballet class. She asked Tito what to do. He advised, "Give them breakfast."

My brother knows more about the Panamanian situation from a personal, as well as business, point of view. In 1958 he was working on his venture of prefabricated housing in Panama. The Panamanians involved included the son of Ernesto de la Guardia Navarro, who served as Panama's president from 1956 to 1960. My brother says the product was good and the contacts were excellent, but the guarantee of buyers had been overblown. When yet another Panamanian revolution threatened, he was advised to leave the country for his own safety.

And guess who advised him about the revolution? Tito Arias's

THE PICTURE PAGE

"It's always fair weather when good fellows get together," and C.C.C. is noted for its "goo fellows" of both sexes. Here you see a few as proof of the statement . . .

Upper left (l. to r.) at the Weissmuller Testimonial Dinner: Gene Fowler, John Montague, Bo C. Roos and Noll Gurney. Upper right Johnny Weissmuller accepting Helm Foundation Trophy from Bill Schroeder while AP Sports Writer Bob Myers looks on. All of Johnny' numerous swimming championship medals were given to the Foundation, where they will be on permanent display. Center left: Dr. Harr Camras and wife at a Square Dance. Center: Carolyn Roos Clark dances with her grandfather, Mr. Holmes. Center right: Jerry Ehrlich and wife entertain the former's parents at the St. Patrick's party. Lower left: Jimmy Hogan and Mrs. Bo Roos greet a friend at one o the Club's social events. Lower center: From the recent Valentine Party, Milton Wershow is seen dancing with an unidentified partner while directly in back of them are the Club's most constant dancers, Mr. and Mrs. Myron Winton. Lower right: Master and pupil . . Jack Gage and Jerry Namar swinging in synchronization.

*The front page of the California Country Club monthly magazine called
"TEE TATTLER". The picture in the center shows my grandfather
Holmes and I dancing at one of the Club's many parties.*

brother! Ironically, the person plotting the revolution against President Ernesto de la Guardia Navarro was Tito Arias himself! In her autobiography Fonteyn wrote that from the second year of their marriage, Tito was absorbed in his idea for a revolution, his sixth, in Panama. She said that Tito discussed the revolution "openly and amusingly with many people in London" and, "Tito's favourite plot ... was the idea of a masked ball at which all the male guests would be invited to go dressed as the President ... When the party reached full swing the real President would be unobtrusively hustled away, and taken out of the country aboard a yacht, preferably Errol Flynn's to add colour to the coup."

In 1958 Tito resigned his ambassadorship and plotted again, but promised Margot it would be his last revolution. He fled the country before he was caught.

Meanwhile the authorities found letters from John Wayne to Tito detailing financial Panamanian operations, leading them to believe that Duke was underwriting some of the sedition. Duke denied it vehemently, claiming that Tito never talked about a revolution, and that the letters referred to investments in Panama, not a revolution. My brother says the people who put together the shrimp boat deals were Bob and Jean McGrath, who operated as the Panama brokers. Although it has been claimed that Dad got Duke into the shrimp boat deal and the Venezuelan partnership, my brother says Dad would never have advised it. Duke's involvement was his own idea.

In 1979 the government of Panama gave John Wayne their highest civilian honor, the Order of Vasco Nuñez de Balboa, in recognition of his forty years of service to the country.

As I said before, the business got very complex!

Ted and I with Mom and Dad "taking a break" in
the Polo Lounge of the Beverly Hills Hotel

CHAPTER 12

WHAT HAVE YOU DONE FOR ME LATELY?

As the old story goes, a public relations representative gets his client the cover story on *Time* magazine one day only to have the client start harassing him the very next day with, "Okay. Yesterday I got the cover of *Time* magazine, but what have you done for me *lately*?"

We had clients like that. Some knew nothing about business. Maria Riva says her mother, Marlene Dietrich, said, "There *must* be money in the bank. Look at all these blank checks we have!" Others looked to Dad to just handle it all. And then there were a few who were active participants in how their money was spent.

Ben Hecht once called Hollywood "an Aladdin's Lamp of a town, and whichever way you rub it, a genie jumps out and makes sport of the laws of gravity and sanity."

Many clients expected Dad to work miracles with their finances and act like a genie with a magic lamp. When he rubbed the lamp and prosperity spewed out, he was a "good" manager. When the big bucks were coming in, and all the bills were being paid, and there was even money left over for investments in the future, my father was "good," sometimes even "brilliant." On the other hand, when the lamp was rubbed and the money that fueled the lamp was producing a negative cash flow, he was a "bad" manager. Some of his clients thought it would just take moving a few decimal points around to get them out of trouble.

Cooking the books was a grand Hollywood tradition (and *still* is, according to some big lawsuits), which we didn't go for. And if an investment deal went sour, Dad was definitely "bad" even though they knew practically every investment carried some risk.

Our clients liked to be helped—in fact, they liked to be coddled—but they didn't like to be told by their business manager that they were spending more than they were making. When more money started going out than was coming in, and Dad had to tell them to cool it, tighten their budget, or sell assets, he was a "bad" business manager.

My father maintained close relationships with all of his clients; sometimes, I think, too close. Part of the business, though, was keeping stars' egos stroked twenty-four hours a day. Managing a stable of superegos was no easy task, and often the lines between friendship and business became blurred.

A good example of that was Johnny Weissmuller, who once said Dad *kept* him from going broke and in the end accused Dad of *making* him broke. In their article in *Cosmopolitan* magazine Kay Mulvey and Marion Frey wrote of Johnny's extravagances that he "used to buy cars to match his suits (and) supported several night clubs single-handed." In his biography, *Tarzan, My Father*, Weissmuller's son admitted that "in fairness to Roos, I must say that my dad was somewhat irresponsible with money, and for years Bö had been telling him to slow down. Johnny Weissmuller never took advice from anybody." He also wrote, "I remember well both Dad and Beryl talking about the heyday of the Hollywood Rat Pack, when they lived high on the hog and enjoyed the best of everything."

At some point, Dad's "kids" had to grow up when it came to money; some never did. When clients got into debt, Dad would sometimes lend them money, with their house or other property as collateral. In Dad's files I found lots of promissory notes from Weissmuller and others for money Dad had lent them that were never paid back. For sure, Dad was a tough businessman, and he sometimes foreclosed on properties to get his money back. That to

Harriet Parsons with her Mother, the famous Hollywood
"gossip" columnist, Louella Parsons.

him was business—certainly not theft or fraud. (Incidentally, in 2004 the Tarzan films starring Johnny Weissmuller and Maureen O'Sullivan were made into a DVD boxed set from Warner Home Video. Who knew DVDs and their profit potential when the films were being made from 1932 to 1942?)

When it comes down to it, there are all kinds of mischief a client can get into and a business manager can't control. Clients are adults, after all. Want a credit card? Sure. Anybody can get a credit card. New car? Why not? Buy several. Go to clubs and restaurants and run up big bills? How could you not pay them? Few stars had the clout of Marlene Dietrich, who was shocked to be presented with a bill in a restaurant. She just waved the waiter away, saying, "What's this? Take it away. It's enough that I am here."

In a recent article in the *New York Times* with the headline "Making Sure Hollywood's Nouveau Riche Stay Riche," Andrew

Dad with Edna Skelton (first wife of Red Skelton).

Blackmun, a current Manhattan business manager, cautions that when he thinks a client is making a bad decision, he puts his reasoning in writing, or "When they're down and out, some lawyer's going to come knocking at your door to try to recoup their lost fortune."

Not everyone was convinced that the business was tough. Every time a deal fell through or a suspicion was raised, somebody started a rumor. For instance, one of director Frank Borzage's wives was convinced that Dad was stealing from him, taking his money. I always said some of these women didn't know their peas from their potatoes when it came to business.

On the other hand, Dad had his staunch supporters. I have a clipping in my files that I believe is from one of the trade papers that reported, "Poison tongues once tried to undermine Red Skelton's faith in Bö ... Red sent for the world's leading firm of company auditors and asked them to examine his records ... The investigation took months ... Red was informed that in the 20 years that Bö Roos had nursed his affairs and his millions, only one item of 178 dollars marked 'Skelton expenses' should have been charged to Bö's personal account ... Red proudly told the poison tongue waggers the result, then paid the auditors' bill—19,500 dollars! ... "It was worth every dollar to prove to Bö's enemies how wrong they were," said Red."

Another fan of my dad's was Edna Skelton. She and Red remained cordial after their divorce, and she continued as co-owner, producer, and co-writer of his shows, as well as overseeing his career and their financial affairs, which were very much intertwined. She was one of the top women executives in the entertainment industry at that time, making $4,500 a week. When she met my dad at a party, she said she wanted no part of a business manager. She was convinced that many of them made a living just on kickbacks from any transactions they made for their clients. But she turned to Dad when she and Red needed tax advice. She was quoted by Richard English in the *Saturday Evening Post* as saying, "I'd never want to be on the spot of having

One of the last photos taken of June Haver MacMurray, with me, at a charity benefit in the Beverly Hills Hotel, about a year before her death.

to apologize to Red for what I did with his money. He wouldn't care, but I do."

Edna especially appreciated Dad's loyalty to his clients. Once he found an actor who was talented, but broke. To help him out he got together several of his clients to back the man until he got on his feet, keeping the actor's financial situation from the studios. Edna and Red had struggled to make it in their early years, so she was particularly sensitive to the problems struggling performers faced.

Harriet Parsons was another fan of ours. She was the gossip columnist Louella Parsons's daughter and one of the few women in Hollywood who was a successful producer. In the same *Saturday Evening Post* article she said, "I know a lot of people say he's in the mention business—you mention it, he's in it. But what's the use of going to a doctor if you won't take his advice?" When one of our deals fell through, and both we and clients lost money, Parsons understood. "We went in with our eyes open ... He told us it was a gamble."

Almost all of Dad's clients followed his advice to invest in real estate, which he thought was safest. He was convinced that it was a good hedge against inflation and that Beverly Hills in particular would be a booming town.

One of our longest personal and client relationships was with Fred MacMurray. Now, there was a client Dad really enjoyed. Fred was very involved in his own business affairs and a real participant when it came to handling his money.

It's interesting how Fred's career got going. According to Sheilah Graham in her memoir *Hollywood Revisited,* Carole Lombard helped to mastermind it, after the two of them starred in a couple of movies together. He was making only $200 a week at the time. Carole sent him to Palm Springs to wait while she pulled some strings. Fred got more and more nervous, but finally she called to tell him the studio would give him a new contract. Sheila wrote, "He called to tell me. What a contract! From $200 to $2,000 a week!" Sheila said, "Fred still has most of it. His friends had to pay for the lighting when they played tennis on his court." Mitch Leisen said, "Fred MacMurray held on to a buck like it was an endangered species."

Over the years Fred's career had its ups and downs. He started playing saxophone in a touring band in the 1920s and 1930s and moved on to play in a Broadway musical and in B-movie roles in Hollywood until he showed his acting chops as the crooked insurance man in *Double Indemnity* opposite Barbara Stanwyck. His box office appeal went up again after he started making Disney

*June MacMurray looking on, as husband
Fred MacMurray practices for next hunting trip.*

Fred and June MacMurray on their Ranch, Twin
Valley Ranch, in Healdsburg, California.

movies such as *The Absent-Minded Professor* and *The Shaggy Dog*
and then started a twelve-year run as the wise father in TV's *My*
Three Sons.

No matter what his income was, Fred kept his eye on the
bottom line. In 1942, his earnings were almost $300,000 a year. In
1945 they had jumped to $400,000, and they kept on climbing.
By 1962 three of his pictures had grossed $32 million, much of it
from percentage deals.

At one time, he was listed as one of the ten richest men in
America. He always pulled an "Aw shucks" modest routine when
someone brought that up and said it was an exaggeration. He would
admit that he had "made a few little investments here and there."
His "little investments," many of which were made on the advice of
my dad, included factories, oil drilling, a sweater factory, marketing

prunes, hotels, country clubs, and a cannery. He excelled in real estate investments. At one time they reputedly consisted of most of Wilshire Boulevard, one of the major, most elegant thoroughfares of Los Angeles. It included the Bryson Hotel and Apartments, which were immortalized by Raymond Chandler in his novels, including *Lady in the Dark*. Property changed hands a lot, but Fred's ranch in northern California stayed in his family for more than fifty years. The ranch covered 1,700 acres by 1941 and had been purchased a few acres at a time over a period of years. The cost totaled about $500,000. He transformed the few homesteads into a working cattle ranch he named the Twin Valley Ranch. He kept a book, *Practical Farming for Beginners*, by the fireplace and loved to ride around on his jeep, working with the hired hands. Years later, after Fred's death the family sold it to the Gallo Wine Company for $6 million and donated much memorabilia from the early history of the ranch as well as family possessions to Sonoma County to help preserve some of its history.

Fred's spending allowance was somewhere around $50 a week, and he often had a couple dozen uncashed allowance checks. I don't think he ever asked for more. His hobbies were fishing and hunting, and his expenses centered around buying sporting equipment.

When Fred married June Haver in 1951, my parents were witnesses at the simple civil ceremony at the Ojai Valley Inn. The honeymoon consisted of "motoring" toward Jackson Hole, Wyoming, where Fred was due to film a movie. Along the way, they planned to sightsee the West, including the Grand Canyon and Bryce Canyon, staying in motels along the way, hardly the lavish display you would expect from a big movie star.

June had appeared in many 1940s musicals, including *The Dolly Sisters* with Betty Grable. She broke her contract in 1953 and was a novice for six months at the Sisters of Charity convent in Kansas. When she returned to Hollywood, she bumped into the recently widowed MacMurray. Their marriage lasted thirty-seven years, until his death.

Jeannette MacDonald and husband Gene Raymond.
I have a nice note from Jeanette, saying she wishes they had taken
dad's advice so they could be as rich as Fred MacMurray.

June and my mother were both Geminis, with their birthdays just two days apart, and celebrated with an annual party.

Throughout the years, Fred and June were such good friends to my family and me. When it came time to close the offices of Beverly Management Corporation, I was president and June was vice president of the operation. Their generosity and caring after my father died was greatly appreciated.

June suffered from hepatitis, and Al Marsella told me how much she cherished Dad's always visiting her through the years when she was hospitalized because of her attacks. She said she would wake up and find him sitting there. Dad always visited friends in the hospital and would take flowers and a big box of candy for the nurses. Al also said that a day or two before June died from other causes, she told him, "I never knew about suffering until now." How sad, but thankfully she did not have to keep suffering.

June and I remained close friends, and included in this book is a photo of the two of us together, taken a short while before she died in July 2005. Known for her sunny disposition over the years, June's obituary in the *Los Angeles Times* described her as "So upbeat that friends were known to greet her with, 'Cheer down, June.'"

After Fred died in 1991, their twin daughters, Katie and Laurie, were a great comfort to June, and they are carrying on with her many business affairs. Katie works for Gallo Wines, which named one of their new wines Twin Valley. We still share some investments with June's estate. Fred's children from his first wife Lillian, were Bob, who lives with his family in Honolulu, and Susan, who lives with her family in the San Fernando Valley.

Dad had an assortment of investments. One was buying 18 percent of the Island Holiday Hotel chain in Hawaii, which included the Maui Palms at Kahului, the Coco Palms Lodge on Kauai, and the Kona Palms on the Big Island. His fellow investors were Duke and Fred MacMurray. The press claimed that the threesome were now "big Hawaii Hotel men." Fred had filmed

The Caine Mutiny in the islands, and John Wayne had made *Big Jim McLain* there. Duke was married at Kona to his third wife, Pilar Palette.

Dad liked the Hollywood Athletic Club, where John Wayne and Ward Bond were active and rowdy members. My brother, Bö, remembers, "My dad was a pal until I was able to compete in athletics, at which time he was close but never the same in competition than one day after I was out of the navy and after I had begun to work for BMC. I asked him for a game of squash at the club. I thought I was pretty good. Two games later, I found myself without one single point. I was way over my head from that moment and began to learn respect." One of my brother's fondest memories, though, is the day he beat Dad at golf and received a lot of Dad's respect in return.

Famed Hollywood publicist Warren Cowan remembers Dad as "a very special and wonderful man ... he was extremely helpful to us in our arranging a golf tournament for his and our client, Frank Borzage. The Frank Borzage Invitational Motion Picture Charity Golf Tournament became the first event ever where a celebrity sponsored a sports event for charity. With Bö's help, we secured the Fox Hills Golf Club in Culver City for the one day tournament. To it came every major star in the business (Gable, Mickey Rooney, Astaire, Crosby, Hope, Sinatra, even Marilyn Monroe as 'official scorekeeper')."

There were three country clubs for which Dad put together the financing. The ill-fated Cabana Club was a beach club and is covered in Chapter 11.

The California Country Club, a golf club, had no members and a deserted clubhouse in 1951. Dad put together a combine with Frank Borzage, John Wayne, Fred MacMurray, Mitchell Leisen, and himself to buy, remodel, and operate it. The investment was around $200,000, and they sold it for $1,050,000. Columnist Irv Kupcinet described it as a "killing" with the 25 percent capital gains tax covering their initial investment, leaving them with a healthy profit to split among themselves.

The Westside Tennis Club was not as successful. Tennis wasn't as classy as golf at that time. Dad tried to talk the members into buying the property, but they wouldn't agree, so the property was sold. For years afterward, former members would say, "We should have listened to Bö Roos and bought the club."

Although Dad would have liked a perfect batting average, it didn't happen. Tommy Lasorda once said that when you're in the pros, winning is all that matters, and that held true for business managers as well as baseball players.

CHAPTER 13

STICKS & STONES

Of all Dad's clients, the biggest were probably John Wayne, Fred MacMurray, Johnny Weissmuller, and Red Skelton. The wealthiest was Fred MacMurray, whose estate was valued at $500 million when he died. Reportedly, John Wayne's was around $30 million. Johnny Weissmuller died "broke." I don't know about Red Skelton.

There have been a couple of negative statements about my father's handling of some of his stars money in one of the books covering John Wayne's life.

I have thought about the differences between men like Wayne and Skelton and MacMurray.. Each one was a star, had a long career, and made fortunes. So why did Fred leave so much more than the others?

Fred's needs were simple, his expenses minimal. He and Dad enjoyed business—talking about it, coming up with ideas, analyzing results. (See Chapter 12.) Fred listened to advice. He didn't always take it, but he listened. With Fred, Dad spent his time concentrating on business. Fred's wives, Lily (who passed away) and his second wife, June Haver, were not extravagant in any way. June was very realistic and straightforward about her movie career. She said, "I had ten good years" and did not expect to live the expensive life of a star forever. We had a financial relationship with the MacMurrays until Fred died in 1990 and June passed away in 2005.

Fred was famous for his frugality. I got a kick out of Howard Keel's autobiography, *Only Make Believe,* in which he wrote about being introduced to Fred during the start party (where the cast meets before shooting begins) for *Callaway Went Thataway.* Howard told Fred, "I already know you ... I'm that skinny kid that used to park your car in front of Paramount. I used to keep it all nice and clean, and you never tipped me one dime." That was in stark contrast to people like Frank Sinatra, who supposedly carried only $100 bills for tipping.

Johnny was 180 degrees opposite of Fred. His son, Johnny Weissmuller Jr., in his biography of his father, *Tarzan, My Father,* says, "I have heard so many different stories and descriptions of Bö Roos ... Mike Oliver ... swears that Roos was nothing but a good and faithful friend and manager to Johnny Weissmuller, as well as to the other stars in his stable." He was very perceptive when he also wrote, "... you must understand that when you talk about being 'penniless' in Hollywood circles, it does not mean that you have no capital assets. It just means that sometimes you can't pay the gardener ... Dad still had property interests."

I was quoted in that book as saying about Johnny, "The biggest problem ... as I see it, was the fact that he and his wife kept spending money and wanting more. And it simply wasn't there. I think Dad just got tired of loaning them money all the time and knowing that he wasn't going to get it back ... I remember that Dad tried and tried to keep Weissmuller from spending so much. He carried him for years, loaning him money. I found lots of notes in Dad's files, signed by Johnny Weissmuller, which were never paid back." I understand Johnny Senior's basic income in his later years came from 15 percent of the proceeds from sales of *The Jungle Jim* television series (which ran from 1948 to 1955) and limited personal appearances. Ben Newman said, "He hadn't worked in a long time," an occupational hazard in the entertainment industry. The residue in assets was not enough to handle the fallout from five wives and a lifetime of lavish spending. (See Chapter 12.)

Red was a spender (see Chapter 10), making up for very impoverished early years. He was one of the most versatile of our clients, adapting to every medium from minstrel shows to television. He wasn't totally naive when it came to business, such as when he insisted on retaining rights to his shows in the age of television. Red also made a substantial amount on his paintings and sales of tapes from his television show. Red's first wife, Edna, a longtime client, was very savvy financially and deserves credit with Dad for conserving a lot of Red's assets.

Duke wanted money and all the things it could buy, but his real love was films more than anything. In her memoir *John Wayne, My Father,* his daughter Aissa says he'd complain about money, then go out and buy Pilar a $5,000 dress or buy Aissa a Porsche for the Christmas she turned sixteen. Three marriages, seven kids, trust funds for everyone, family on the payroll, a jet, a helicopter, a yacht, film financing (remember the Alamo?) all added up. (See Chapter 8.) Pilar described a Christmas shopping spree, saying, "We were like two children having fun ... and soon spent $20,000 to $30,000." You need a lot of income and cash on hand to cover that kind of fun. Before Duke left BMC, he told Dad dramatically, "I have given you millions. What have you done with my money?" The answer, not so dramatic: the flow of money *out* the door.

One very critical account of Dad failed to provide any details about the arbitration proceedings between Duke and Dad and even got the arbitrator's name wrong. At any rate, the arbitrator faulted both of them on their communication habits, or lack thereof. (See Chapter 8.)

That was true. At BMC contracts were made with a handshake, not a written contract, and clients didn't always understand the ramifications. Ben Newman remembers Dad's habit of coming to meetings early and "having to leave" when time ran out or the proceedings bored him. Sometimes questions were left unanswered. Often clients preferred having a drink to bothering with details. It was, "Bö, just take care of it."

That was the case with Duke. He was a lot more interested in making movies than in financial details. He made dozens of B Westerns in the '30s that were often churned out at the rate of one a week, and somebody counted up eighty-two feature-length films from 1939 to 1972. From 1972 to his death in 1979, he made several more, including *Rooster Cogburn* in 1975 and *The Shootist* in 1976. He figured if he needed more money, he could always make another film. Duke's love of movies impressed Peter Bogdanovich, who wrote in *Who The Hell's In It* that as "part of his deal" Duke got 35-mm prints of almost all his movies, including *Stagecoach*. Because the original negative of that film had been lost or destroyed, Peter suggested that Duke donate the print to the nonprofit American Film Institute. Duke liked that it would be a tax write-off and that *Stagecoach* was saved.

A few allegations were just ridiculous. One critic wrote that Dad was broke in 1957—totally untrue. Another said Dad spent a month in Japan having sex with geisha girls. If my information is correct, the code of behavior for geisha girls is very strict about sex: they don't have it.

Some clients pointed to Dad's "money-losing" propositions, not understanding that some tax shelters were *purposely* money losing. We wanted to increase a client's expenses, thereby getting him into a lower tax bracket so he could retain more of his income. For example, there are oil wells that were not producing much at one time but were a tax write-off. When income was needed, the oil wells were either sold or refurbished. Some of them are still producing to this day, more than thirty years after my father's death.

My favorite complaint is the clients who "didn't know," even though every check and document had to be signed by the client as well as BMC. One claimed that Dad had borrowed against an insurance policy without the client's knowledge. I can just see an insurance company advancing cash without a client's approval! Most clients knew what they wanted—more money—and looked to Dad to figure out how to raise it. That often involved mortgaging property, drawing on other assets, and other techniques. Then they claimed to be "unaware" that there was payback time.

If the accusations were on the level some people reported, I have no doubt there would have been major lawsuits. After all, a couple of the accusers were high-powered, high-priced attorneys, and they *know* how to sue; that's their business.

Yes, there was a lawsuit for $40,000 from Gene Raymond that was decided in Dad's favor, but legal fees ate up the proceeds. The biggest altercation was the arbitration, not lawsuit, with John Wayne, and it was resolved by Duke owing Dad more than $66,000. (See Chapter 8.)

Much of the criticism Dad received was from secretaries who were maternal, almost ferocious in protecting their bosses. The same was true for wives and even kids (some of whom were barely born when BMC was in business). If there were money problems, it had to be somebody's fault, and what better target than the business manager? After Duke left BMC and appointed and later terminated his son-in-law, Don La Cava, as his business manager, his wife, Pilar, wrote in *John Wayne—My Life with the Duke* that Duke asked her "if I wanted to take control of his remaining investments and future earnings," which shocked her because "No one knew better than Duke how little I understood business." If a wife brought up questions about a star's finances, Dad usually dismissed it with "They don't know much about business." Maybe he should have listened. And maybe his clients should have listened more to him.

Most of our clients were affiliated with the movie business, which changed drastically over the years. According to Kathleen Sharp in her book *Mr. and Mrs. Hollywood*, during the Depression 75 percent of the nation went to the movies once a week, but by 1950 only 20 percent took in a movie weekly. As Ezra Goodman wrote in his book *The Decline & Fall of Hollywood*, "in the final years of the 1950s, the Hollywood dream factory became a nightmare. The plush, lush old days had gone forever," overshadowed by television. Most of our clients' careers and incomes were adversely affected. In 1957 headlines read: "The American Federation of Television and Radio Artists meets to discuss yet another threat to profitability: Pay TV." Television affected magazines as well. *Look* magazine folded after thirty-four years, as did *Life* magazine in 1972. The headlines read: "Advertisers have fled for the lure of TV."

Dad had more than 100 clients during his years as a business manager. If they had money problems *using* Dad's advice, I wonder where they would have been *without* it. I think some of them were children looking for a fairy godmother to turn their income into wealth or a magician to pull it out of a hat, rather than a business manager operating in the real world. Obviously most clients stayed with us and were satisfied with our services, or we wouldn't have stayed in business for so long. I know many of them retired gracefully, having relied on Dad's advice, especially concerning real estate investments, and that they or their heirs are enjoying the proceeds to this day.

Sam Goldwyn once said, "Hindsight is always 20-20." Looking back you can see instances of what "coulda, woulda, shoulda" been done or not (including nipping some of the rumors in the bud). On the whole I think what BMC did made sense.

Frank Capra said there's one word that best describes Hollywood and that's "nervous." It's as good a word as any in describing Hollywood's business affairs and a star's income—NERVOUS!

CHAPTER 14

FUN & FROLIC

Someone said that wherever Bö Roos went, fun followed. There was always something going on when he was around, and if things got too quiet or serious, he'd create some kind of excitement to liven things up. Parties seemed to erupt in the office, at our house, on the boats, in Catalina, and Mexico and anyplace else on land, sea, and in the air where he happened to be. There was always something to celebrate—anniversaries, birthdays, guests in town, a premiere, a new client, an old client, a prospective deal, or milestones for friends and family.

He was inventive in creating kicks. For instance, once he arranged for a train to be put on a barge so he could say he went on a train to Catalina. Since Catalina is an island, surrounded by water and accessible only by boat or plane, that was quite a news-making first. That turned out so well that he and his cronies in the Punting and Sailing Club stuck a sailboat on a truck so they could say they sailed from Beverly Hills to landlocked Las Vegas. One of his craziest pranks was creating a waterfall in the St. Francis Hotel in San Francisco with the help of Johnny Weissmuller and a fire hose. God only knows about the stunts they pulled that we never knew about! I do know they hired a hearse to take them to a fancy party at the San Francisco mayor's house.

The Cocoanut Grove at the Ambassador Hotel, which opened in 1921, was a favorite spot for decades for the family to celebrate

Above: The internationally renowned Cocoanut Grove provided a glimpse of the splendor of Hollywood. The Grove became the symbol of the silent era's glamorous lifestyle.

At right: Bob Cummings and companion make an appearance at the Troc. The club's official opening coincided with the opening of A Midsummer Night's Dream at the Hollywood Bowl, but devotees flooded the club after the performance.

We all strutted our stuff at Night Clubs such as the Cocoanut Grove, Mocambo, and Trocadero.

special events and to entertain for business. It was the hot spot for Hollywood celebrities to see and be seen. The women would be dressed to the nines, especially the movie stars, who could borrow deluxe wardrobes from the studios. The men wore tuxes to the clubs, and as everyone knows, it doesn't take a Fred Astaire or Cary Grant to look good in a tux! At one time, the table centerpieces at the Grove featured dolls made in the likenesses of movie stars. We were there so often that I collected quite a few. Unfortunately, they were lost in one of our moves. Today, they're valued as a very scarce collector's item.

We saw all the big acts at the Grove, including Bing Crosby, Phil Harris, Merv Griffin, Judy Garland, Tommy Dorsey, Rudy Vallee, and our clients The Andrews Sisters. Society columnist Cobina Wright reported on the Andrews show, saying that the girls were sporting a different-colored poodle cut and that their smooth, synchronized singing and the appealing brand of their humor was as much their own as the song "Rum and Coca Cola." She also gave details on the party that Dad had thrown for them and for Edith Head, who designed their gowns. She called Dad "one of the most popular men in Hollywood."

Freddy Martin and his band were regulars at the Grove. He and I had back-to-back birthdays, so when he was playing there, we'd make a point to celebrate together with a champagne toast.

The Grove was also headquarters for many industry events such as the Academy of Television Arts & Sciences awards banquet, where our client Red Skelton won the Emmy for best comedy show in 1951 against a stellar list of competitors. (See Chapter 10.) According to Ambassador Hotel historian Margaret Burk in her book, *Are the Stars Out Tonight?* the Academy Awards for motion pictures were presented in the Grove six times, including the first presentation of the gold Oscar statuette.

My son Denis remembers the Grove well and how he realized at one point how much power Dad had in the entertainment and social world. Denis wrote that on the night of his sister Cathy's debutante ball at the Beverly Wilshire Hotel, "We were

At right: The Mocambo in all of its supercharged glory. Dancing around its flaming red stiped columns might be Judy Garland and David Rose, Lana Turner and Tony Martin, Lucille Ball and Desi Arnaz and Clark Gable and Carole Lombard—on a single night!

Above: Jimmy Stewart fascinates Ginger Rogers at the Café Trocadero, official playground for Hollywood stars; thanks to L.A.'s blue laws, Sunday night became the night at the Troc.

At right: George Jessel and Lois Andrews relax in the subdued light of the Mocambo. It was probably the only subdued thing about the place.

They would always put a table on the dance floor for a Bö Roos party.

all in white jackets, ties, very formal. At the last minute, my grandfather asked, 'What would you like to do?' It was already 9 P.M., and I popped up with 'the Righteous Brothers are in town at the Cocoanut Grove.' Grandfather said, 'No problem.' Off we go, probably 8 to 12 of us. The Maitre d' at the Grove greeted us, 'Mr. Roos! Mr. Roos! One minute.'

"All of a sudden the band stopped playing. The lights went up. The stage slowly retracted about 10 feet backwards. From the far end of the room, we saw two huge tables being carried by waiters down the aisle. They set them down right in front of the stage, then set the tables with white table cloths and complete set ups. We filed all the way down to the front, and the minute the last person sat down the band started playing again, and the Righteous Brothers came out and sang. This was 1964, and they were the number one music group in the U.S., but the show was delayed for my Grandfather. It was completely overwhelming, and I finally realized how much clout my Grandfather had."

Glamour oozed at other nightspots such as the Trocadero owned by *Hollywood Reporter* publisher Billy Wilkerson, Don the Beachcomber's, the Tropics on Rodeo Drive, the Cinegrill, the Biltmore Bowl, the Hollywood Palladium, Earl Carroll's Theater, and so many more. Stars were expected to go out on the town and did. Part of the attraction of going to these places was seeing Gable dancing with Carole Lombard, or William Powell with Jean Harlow, Joan Crawford and Franchot Tone, and many more glamorous people in and out of show business.

Dad took me to all the top nightspots and restaurants in town starting when I was still a teenager. I think he liked showing me off, but he also wanted to take me to the best places first to be sure I wouldn't be too starry eyed or easily impressed when it came to dating.

Whenever we went to fancy places, we always got a ringside seat if Dad was with us. If not, he arranged it so we would. I remember getting seated ringside at the Copacabana in New York

PIES SERVED WITH
WHIPPED CREAM,
CHEESE OR
ICE CREAM,
5c EXTRA

—Boston Cream Pie 10   Devil's Food Cake 10c
—Banana Cream Pie 10c   Apple Sauce Cake 10c
)AY—Walnut Cream Pie 10c   Chocolate Cake 10c
Y—Blackbottom Pie 10c   Spice Cake 10c
Butterscotch Pie 10c   Creole Cake 10c
Y—Martha Washington Pie 10c   Fudge Cake 10c
—Lemon Cream Pie 10c   Cocoanut Cake 10c

MAY WE SUGGEST THESE TEMPTING

Dessert Specials

IN ITSELF
a Split
us Dessert
5c

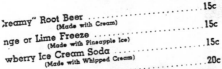

'reamy" Root Beer 15c
          (Made with Cream)
nge or Lime Freeze 15c
          (Made with Pineapple Ice)
wberry Ice Cream Soda 15c
          (Made with Whipped Cream)
                                                          20c
) Sundae ....
          (Whipped Cream and Sliced Almonds)
                                                          20c
Pecan Nut" Sundae ....
          (Plenty Whipped
Sundae ....
          (Plenty Whipped
ned Fresh Strawberry
          (with Plenty Whip
us Roman Regular Rob

Double Thick Malted Milk (Any
We Use Ice Cream, Sweet Mi
Milk Shake—Extra Thick or Thi
Ice Cream Soda, Whipped Cre
Ice Cream, Extra Rich: Vanilla,
Sundae: (Choc., Strawberry, P
Fresh Orange or Lime Freeze
Frosted Creamy Root Beer ...

*Simon's Drive-In was a popular spot in Beverly Hills, in the 1940's and
1950's. Note the prices of the food. Great desserts for ten cents.*

City when Frank Sinatra was early in his career. His fans went wild over him. He came over and sat with us. I was not impressed with the man, but his voice was fantastic.

Even going out for ice cream seemed to be a lot of fun. Mom and Dad's first date was having a Brown's Special Chocolate Ice Cream Soda at an ice cream parlor. I don't know what a soda cost when they were dating, but when I was a teen, the price was 10 cents at our favorite hangout, the Simon's Drive-In at Wilshire Boulevard and Linden in Beverly Hills. Simon's had a string of twenty-seven restaurants in the Los Angeles area at that time and was billed as "The West's Largest Restaurant Chain." I have a menu that lists pies, cakes, ice cream sundaes, and drinks (lemonade, buttermilk, juices, and the like) and, surprisingly, local bottled beer for 15 cents and Eastern Bottled Beer for 20 cents. As far as we were concerned, Simon's was a Beverly Hills hot spot.

At the time, one of my friends and sometime date was Bill McEdwards who later changed his name to Blake Edwards and became well known as a director/producer/writer and married Julie Andrews. His credits include *Days of Wine and Roses*, *Breakfast at Tiffany's*, and *The Pink Panther* series. I think part of why Bill came to the house so often was that he hoped my father could help him in his acting ambitions. My brother says Bill thanks him whenever they see each other because one day when he jumped into our swimming pool, he hit his head, causing a concussion and gaining him a draft deferment.

Dad got involved in the nightclub business at one point, helping put together the Pirate's Den, where I understood Merv Griffin got his start performing. The club's Council of Great Pirate Chiefs was listed on the masthead as Fred MacMurray, Jimmie Fidler, Johnny Weissmuller, Tony Martin, Rudy Vallee, Bob Hope, Ken Murray, and Bing Crosby. You could get jailed or ticketed for any goofy reason and had to perform your way out of jail by doing something like screaming the loudest. It was a lot of noisy fun while it lasted.

Around that time, during the early years of World War II, Mom and I volunteered at the Hollywood Canteen. I was only nineteen at the time, but the servicemen seemed so very young and unsophisticated to me. So many were away from their homes for the first time in their lives. We danced with them, served sandwiches and coffee, helped write letters home, admired the photos in their wallets, and just listened to kids who were lonesome for female company. There were always good acts on the stage. Dad helped to book many of them for clients or contacts to mingle, perform, and sign autographs. Everybody was eager to pitch into the war effort, and I remember everything being very wholesome except for one really foul-mouth performance by Sophie Tucker that made everybody uncomfortable.

Our client Frank Borzage directed a movie called *Stage Door Canteen* in 1943 that reminds me so much of the Hollywood Canteen atmosphere. It's sometimes shown on late-night television on classic movie channels. The most remarkable thing about the film is the number of big stars of the era who performed or did cameos, including Benny Goodman, Helen Hayes, Katharine Hepburn, Count Basie, Edgar Bergen, Harpo Marx, Alfred Lunt and Lynne Fontanne, Paul Muni, and so many more.

In addition to nightclubs and restaurants Dad had a string of contacts at hotels all over town. Some were investments, others were kept to put up visitors or as "hideouts" for clients or when it was advantageous for people to think Dad was out of town. They included a bungalow at the Beverly Hills Hotel (next to Howard Hughes's bungalow, site of his many affairs with glamorous movie stars, including Katharine Hepburn),an apartment in the Chateau Marmont in Hollywood, the Bryson Hotel ,an apartment in the California Country Club and the Culver Hotel in Culver City, next to MGM.

We went out a lot, but we frequently entertained at home, too. Mom was a wonderful hostess at innumerable parties at the house, which she made very comfortable and inviting and furnished with some lovely antiques. In particular, Mom outdid herself when she and my father hosted a huge wedding reception for my husband, Ted, and me. Louella Parsons reported in her column that Fred MacMurray's cute mother and Mrs. Red Skelton's mama were there, and that "Fred looks exactly like his mom, and Mrs. Red and her mother might pass for sisters ... John Wayne came with Pilar Pallette. District Attorney Roll and his wife, Lita Baron and Rory Calhoun, and so many others congratulated the newlyweds."

Dad delighted in creating good times for people even when he himself was not present. My son Denis remembers when, being the oldest grandchild, he was the first to be treated to the fruits of Dad's piggy bank proceeds. (See Chapter 15 about piggy banks.) Denis chose a round-the-world trip and wrote that Grandad "notified friends that he wanted me to visit. I started off going west: Hawaii, Fiji, Sydney, Perth, Singapore, Hong Kong, Bangkok. Fortunately, I was well-dressed the day I flew into Bangkok. I didn't know who I was about to meet. So I got into the Customs line to show my passport. When I got in front, two Thai military officers asked me, 'Are you Olsen?' When I said yes, they grabbed me, and I was taken past everybody. All of a sudden I was shaking hands with a line of about 15 people in military uniform and their wives. I didn't know what was going on, but apparently I was a guest of the commanding General of the Thai army! He set me up with a car and driver, hotel, everything. It was quite a surprise. Apparently, Grandad had entertained the General on a yacht with John Wayne and was incredibly overwhelmed with my Grandfather's generosity, and he was returning the favor."

All the socializing necessitated buying gifts of all kinds for clients, prospects, contacts, guests, friends, family, and prizes given out at the clubs. In the 1940s and 1950s BMC spent $50,000 a year on gifts. Unlike most men, Dad loved to shop, as did Red Skelton. I was often deputized to do the shopping, and Mom helped. Beverly Hills stores were (and are) world famous. We spent a lot of money at Ruser's Jewelers. Red Skelton was a tough one to buy for. We'd send him a Christmas present, then he'd top our gift with something else, and we'd feel compelled to go out and get more.

Both Dad and Granddad were generous. Mom was, too, but she would scold Dad all the time for overspending. She was right, but it didn't keep him from having a wonderful time buying things, and she often received lovely gifts from him. I remember when I was in high school Dad and Granddad bought me a '41 Ford convertible, black with red leather seats, supercharged and souped up with a Mercury engine (just like the Beverly Hills cops had). Dad had to get a police permit so I could drive it on the streets. In the 1950s similar models were used for drag racing. Even though I lived just across the street from school, several times I drove the car around the block and parked in the school's back parking lot. The car cost $1,200 and was sold five years later for $1,500. It would be a real classic now!

At times I helped clients select gifts. Once Red Skelton and I picked out a lovely gold angel sitting on a cloud of freshwater pearls with diamonds woven throughout for his wife. Afterward we stopped at the Tropics (just down the street on Rodeo Drive) for a drink, and he gave me a gold heart pendant as a thank-you and said, "From my heart to yours." Another time when we were in New York, Red and I had fun picking out a hat for me so we could stroll down Park Avenue in the Easter parade, followed by the photographers. Fun time.

A very special part of our family's memories were made on Catalina Island, which was an important part of our lives from the time I was five or six. There are many small towns in California, but few are as unique and charming as Avalon on Catalina, a small island off the coast of Southern California. There's a famous song whose lyrics go, "Santa Catalina is awaitin' for me, 26 miles across the sea." Its closeness to the mainland was part of its appeal, but it was also a wonderful getaway and playground. Among its attractions were fantastic fishing, swimming, water sports, sightseeing, ferries, seals, glass-bottom boats, yacht clubs, beautiful dances in the huge Casino building with the Big Bands, buried treasures, movie stars and filmmaking, herds of buffalo (leftovers from a 1920s movie filmed there), and other wildlife.

Early in the 1930s we'd take the big white Steamer from the port of San Pedro for the two-hour voyage to the island. There was usually a trio playing dance music on board the ship. When the Steamer got near to shore, it would be greeted by a flotilla of speedboats racing around it. Some of the speedboats were "Miss Catalinas," beautiful teak speedboats belonging to Avalon's mayor, Al Bombard, a good friend over the years. As the Steamer was docking, kids would be in the water waiting for the passengers to toss money down to them so they could dive for the coins. On shore a "welcome committee" would be waiting with a crowd of people and a small band playing.

We took our place as residents, not tourists, at a house Dad owned on the island. He bought and sold property regularly over the years, the most recent being the house on Catalina Avenue in Avalon. It was so nice just sitting on the front porch of the cottage, enjoying the sunset and watching the lights come on in the homes up in the hills and far off on the mainland, and at night to see the moonlight and stars twinkling across the water. We quickly made friends, and my parents became very close to the Wrigleys of chewing-gum fortune and fame, who were responsible for developing the island. Among our other very good friends were Vince and June Scarramucci, who owned a famous restaurant in town named Scari's.

Part of the attraction of Catalina was the large variety of boats anchored in or sailing in and out of the harbor. There were the little dinghies, rowboats, motorboats, sailboats and plenty of upscale yachts. (Traditionally, a boat becomes a yacht when its length is 40 feet or more.) It wasn't long before Dad bought his first boat—a 35-foot Chris Craft named *Amaroo* (which means "safe harbor"). That was followed by the *Amaroo II*, a larger, 45-foot Chris Craft, and still later the 76-foot *Norwester* bought with John Wayne. Duke eventually bought a 136-foot minesweeper, the *Wild Goose*, his pride and joy, and even sailed it across the

One of Catalina Island's most famous landmarks, the Casino
Ballroom, was completed in 1929 and contains a movie theater
on the ground floor. The Ballroom on the top hosted all of
the big bands including the Kay Kyser band pictured.

The vacation cottage, owned by the Roos family since the early 1930's.

Atlantic. In her autobiography, *John Wayne—My Life with the Duke*, his wife Pilar wrote: "Most of our family vacations were spent aboard the *Norwester* and the *Goose*." Mom and Dad were early members of the Catalina Island Yacht Club, and Ted and I carried on the tradition. The Club just this year celebrated their 84th birthday.

I was convinced that our boats were the best, but I had to admit we had some competition. Among the beautiful boats that anchored in Catalina was director John Ford's sailboat, the *Araner*. People said Ford loved that boat more than his family. It was used for fun, but I also heard that Maureen O'Hara would take notes in shorthand from him aboard the *Araner* about his plans to make *The Quiet Man*. Among the other boats were Humphrey Bogart's *Santana*, Johnny Weissmuller's *Guadalupe* (and later the *Allure*), and Errol Flynn's *Sirocco* that he bought for $24,000. Flynn was a born mariner. It was said he could sail a piece of bark across the ocean. All of them were enthusiastic boaters who took great pride in their vessels.

Dad's first boat, the Amaroo, which means "Safe Harbor". Aboard this time is Dad and I with Jim Clark and Duke Woods.

In the early '30s we had no trouble acquiring a mooring in Avalon, and there was lots of room to anchor. As I recall, the harbormaster offered Dad a 45-foot mooring at the purchase price of $50 in Avalon Harbor. It never occurred to Dad to "own" a mooring. (Today, a mooring would cost in the millions.) At the beginning of each summer Dad just distributed a few bottles of Chivas Regal and entertained the harbor guys on board with his special hamburgers with peanut butter in them. Even with the island's small area (about twenty-six miles long), and the size of the city of Avalon (one square mile) with its population (only 2,500 residents as late as the early '90s) we thought that Avalon was too crowded. We boaters would escape to the "Isthmus" (now "Two Harbors"). Many of the movie producers and stars called the Isthmus "the poor man's Hawaiian Islands," and many films were made there, including *Treasure Island, Captains Courageous,* and *Mutiny on the Bounty.* According to Lee Rosenthal in his book *Catalina in the Movies,* "Between 1915 and 1935 ... part or all of over 150 Hollywood movies were filmed on Catalina

The Amaroo II, Dad's second boat. (R.J. Wagner and Natalie Wood chartered her for their first honeymoon.) She was a 45 ft. Chris Craft.

... and in recent decades (it) has been the locale for countless videos, television shows, commercials, and background for scenes for major studio productions such as Roman Polanski's *Rosemary's Baby* and *Chinatown*.

Art La Shelle, Dad's best friend from childhood, owned a large barge in the Isthmus Harbor that was used a lot in the making of movies because the cameramen could shoot off of it into the many caves. Art's brother, Joe La Shelle, was a famous cameraman, and between the filming location, Art's friends and Dad's, and the performers at the Casino, there were always many movie stars around.

After boating and watching films being made, swimming was probably the most popular sport. Johnny Weissmuller had taught my brother and me to swim, and we enjoyed the sport all of our lives. Johnny had a specially built paddleboard that he would use to "aquaplane" by tying a rope around the bow of it and then taking off behind a motorboat. It was a lot harder to handle than today's water skis. My brother and I loved using the board to go out to Bird Rock. Art La Shelle swam to Bird Rock and back every day, without the use of a paddleboard. I remember the day that Al Bombard and Dad tried to do it but gave up before they were halfway there.

Johnny was a fantastic Olympic gold medal swimmer. Once Humphrey Bogart challenged Johnny to a race. Johnny swam and Bogart was in a small outboard, and Johnny won.

Art La Shelle operated and hosted the bar and grill known as Christian's Hut on the Isthmus, which was initially a saloon downstairs and sleeping quarters upstairs that Clark Gable used during the filming of *Mutiny on the Bounty* in 1935. It was named after Gable's role as Fletcher Christian. Art was famous for the luaus he put on that attracted many of his friends from Hawaii as well as the mainland.

Dad's third boat, The Norwester, owned by both Dad and John Wayne together for many years. She was a 76 ft. "all wood" luxury yacht. My husband Ted and I purchased the Norwester in 1973 and enjoyed sailing it to Catalina, Mexico and many points in between.

Mom and Dad, Ted and I, at the Cocoanut Grove in the famous Ambassador Hotel; a favorite place for our family to celebrate special occasions.

Art also was in charge of the entertainment at the Casino, which was built in 1928 and cost $2 million. Its theater seats 1,200, and supposedly as many as 650 can dance in the ballroom at one time. By the late 1930s I would take a girlfriend or a boyfriend over to Catalina. I remember how exciting and romantic it was dancing there with a boyfriend to the music of Count Basie and so many of the "big bands" when I was a teenager and for many years after.. Big Band musicians that performed there regularly included Kay Kayser, Benny Goodman, Freddy Martin, Jan Garber, and so many more.

In the 1950s, Art, Dad, and Duke Wayne, along with several Hollywood celebrities, held a meeting to form the Emerald Bay Yacht Club. One of the guys had arranged for a group of three bagpipers and a drummer to come and play each time someone started to speak and keep playing until he sat down. What clowns! If you can imagine how deafening a sound three pipers and a drummer can make in closed quarters!

There are so many memories about Catalina, including the time Natalie Wood and Robert Wagner chartered the *Amaroo II* for their first honeymoon at the Isthmus. On a sad day in 1981, they spent the weekend on their own 55-foot yacht, the *Splendor*, anchored at the Isthmus, when Natalie fell overboard during the

Our clients "The Andrews Sisters" were a big hit at the Grove,
and of course all over the world in the 1940's.

night and drowned. It was so tragic, made worse by knowing how easily accidents can happen on the water.

On a happier note, we were involved in creating the Garden House Inn on Catalina with our son Jon in the late '80's. The building had been named the Idle Ours and was built by the Mead family in 1923. My husband, Ted, daughter Cathy, and I went over to Catalina to help my son Jon with his plans for transforming it into a ten-room, eleven-bath bed-and-breakfast called Garden House Inn. It became one of the most popular places to stay.

It was sold to the Catalina Island Conservancy in 1992. During that stay on the island I became corresponding secretary for the Santa Catalina Island Woman's Club and a director with the Catalina Island Chamber of Commerce, and wrote for several years for the *Avalon Bay News*.

Newport Beach was also important to the family. Bogie and Jimmy Cagney had docked their boats here, and John Wayne lived here from 1965 to 1979. Many of the stars had second homes in Newport Beach and used it as a quick getaway from the pressures of Hollywood. When the Christian's Hut on Catalina burned down, Art La Shelle opened another one in the Newport Beach area on the Balboa Penninsula.

Ted and I and our children moved to Newport around 1960 and built a house on Balboa Island. My parents lived here in their later years. In 1961 Ted and I joined the Balboa Bay Club, which I understand was built on land used during the war as mooring for a fleet of old schooners that were used for offshore antisubmarine patrol. We bought a 28-foot boat called a Baltic Sea Roamer, christened it the *Harbinger*, and moored it at the club. The boat and the Balboa Bay Club became an enjoyable part of our lives and still is one for me.

One of the highlights was when my daughter Cathy was married. Duke lent us the *Wild Goose* for the ceremony. We

The Pirate's Den, a great nightclub project of Dad's and several of his clients. I have heard that Merv Griffin sang there in his early days.

The Christian's Hut at The Isthmus, Catalina.

were allowed to take only fifty passengers if we went outside the jetty. Cathy wanted to be married "at sea," but we needed to accommodate more guests. We solved that by taking fifty guests out to sea and picking up fifty more at the Balboa Bay Club after the ceremony With 100 guests aboard we cruised Newport Harbor. We had a sumptuous buffet and a three-piece combo, and John Wayne and Pilar waved to us from their dock as the wedding party sailed by.

For many years,(after we acquired the Norwester) we docked the boat outside Ted's and my condominium, with the cruise boats pointing it out as John Wayne's first boat. As they passed by, they would wave and we would wave back. Fun.

When I look back on the times we had over the years, I think, Wow! Fun and frolic indeed!

Pictures of the Bö Roos funeral held at Forest Lawn in Los Angeles and attended by his family, his friends, and many past clients... including John Wayne and Fred MacMurray as honorary pallbearers.

CHAPTER 15

BÖ REMEMBERED

Dad died in August 1973 at the age of sixty-nine from a heart attack at Hoag Hospital in Newport Beach, the end to a series of strokes he suffered starting in May 1967. My parents had lived in Newport Beach only a few months before he passed away.

I was on the phone for three days making arrangements for the funeral. Dealing with the press, planning the service and the burial, and contacting all his friends was exhausting. I lost seven pounds in three days. The service was held at the Church of the Recessional at Forest Lawn. Murray Korda played the violin, and Edward Bates, a good friend from the Vatican, did the eulogy.

The pallbearers included my brother (who was on Catalina when Dad died), John Wayne, Carlos Reyes (who flew in from Mexico), Frank Belcher, Bob Fellows, Dad's brother Art, and Fred MacMurray. It was quite a large affair with family and friends and many of the motion picture people he had managed.

Mike Oliver headlined his front-page column from Los Angeles: "Adios Amigo" and quoted former president of Mexico Miguel Alemán as saying, "Mexico has lost a great friend." In a page-long tribute, he wrote, "Bö Roos' beautiful wife, the petite Billie, braved it all like a bullfighter with tons of flowers covering Forest Lawn in Glendale, cars miles long with friends who had flown in from 360 degrees of the world, and there she stood handsomely with John Wayne, Fred MacMurray ... their daughter Carolyn and his son Bö Roos, Jr. ... The death of Bö Christian Roos is deeply felt in all corners of the world and with our hearts in our hands, we will sign off by using one of his favorite ways of saying goodbye, 'God Bless.'"

The Foreign Friends of Acapulco newsletter said: "OUR BELL TOLLS SADLY ... for the loss in death of another of our longtime members ... the well known, highly respected and admired ... Bö Christian Roos ... who was deep in the affections of those fortunate to know him well ... A real estate magnate of renown, financier and financial advisor to many public figures ... and whose life story is a saga that would top the Horatio Alger novels of yesteryear ... our deepest sympathies."

Obituaries appeared in the foreign press as well as newspapers coast to coast, including the *Los Angeles Times*, the *Los Angeles Herald Examiner*, and the *Hollywood Reporter*. *Daily Variety* reported that Dad "virtually founded the profession of business manager and personal manager." The *New York Times* wrote, "Because of his flamboyant, high-powered and hectic way of life, Bö (pronounced Boo) Roos could have been the model for the movie stereotype of the Hollywood business manager."

Letters and cards poured in from all over, including one from Major General Joseph D. Caldara, who wrote, "I don't know that I ever made plain just how much I admired Bö. He became one of the really dear friends from my service career—and there weren't very many of them. And the older I get, the more I realize just how rare they are in a lifetime."

People at the service reminisced about the times they shared with Dad—business deals, parties, fishing trips, work and play, even the arguments. Several said he would have made a terrific ambassador for the United States. Many said they were glad they had taken his financial advice. Somebody joked that we should put a phone in the coffin because he was *always* on the phone.

People came from many different walks of life to pay their respects, not just clients and business associates. He had been

This was a beautiful gold money clip given to Dad by some of his clients, friends and family, with the following sentiments inscribed on the layers of gold circles: Merry Xmas to Bö Christian Roos, "we love you", "our beloved Bö", from The Duke (John Wayne), Johnny (Johnny Weissmuller), Sheik Ali Alireza, Your Fred (Fred MacMurray), Red, Georgia, goddaughter Valentina and Richard Skelton, Billie, Carolyn and Bö, Jr.

a member of many organizations, including a life member of Masonic Lodge 513, Consistory & Al Malaikah Temple and Knights Templar and almost a dozen clubs that I know of, such as Friars, Variety, Kiwanis, Club de Banqueros de Mexico, Lakeside Golf Club, Outrigger Canoe Club in Honolulu, Emerald Bay Yacht Club, West Side Tennis Club, Aviation Country Club, Big Canyon Country Club, and of course The Old Shoes.

His grandchildren have many fond memories of their grandfather. He kept six silver piggy banks in his dressing room where he would empty his pockets each night. When a piggy bank was full, the money was deposited to an account for each grandchild. When each turned twenty-one, he treated them to a round-the-world trip. (Warren Cowan says he thinks of Dad every night because he picked up Dad's piggy bank ritual for his own family.)

These are some of the memories shared by the family:

My daughter **Cathy Olsen Mylrea**: "Grandfather had a powerful personality and a great charm about him with great love for his family. I am glad I had the opportunity to go along for the ride. He was bigger than life to me as a little girl. When I was in the fifth grade, I'd hear an 'ugga ugga' horn and look up to see a white Cadillac convertible with my grandfather at the wheel. He had a moo horn on the car and a ding-dong bell. He was always dressed to the nines and handsome, with his mustache and gray felt fedora hat, like Clark Gable. He'd say, 'Hi, honey, let's go do something special,' and we'd go off for a hot fudge sundae or to lunch someplace like the Brown Derby or Hamburger Hamlet. He was like a kid himself.

"Once when I was fourteen, my grandparents took me to Mexico City, Taxco, and Acapulco, first class all the way. While Nana rested, we went to a jewelry store, and he bought me seven thin gold bracelets, one for each day of the week. Nana railed against the extravagance; Grandfather winked at me and ignored her. He was a real shopaholic and would buy me Easter dresses at

Saks Fifth Avenue and loved picking up Christmas presents at a toy store with a lemonade tree on Rodeo Drive."

My son **Jon Olsen:** "I remember Sundays at my grandparents' house, too, in and around the swimming pool. My cousins were there a lot, including my great uncle Ed's kids. I was younger than the others, and since we moved to Newport when I was only six, I didn't know him as well as some of the others did, but I remember how kind he was. I had a pet rat who died, and both my grandparents were sympathetic to my loss and let me bury it at the end of the swimming pool.

"When I turned twenty-one, rather than taking a trip around the world, I took the $4,000 that he saved for me and used it as down payment on my first home in Los Osos. I feel a lot of my success in life financially has been due to his indirect influence. When I was a kid, I think he was reaching out to teach me the value of money, independence, and having options in life that that kind of success provides."

Vicki Roos Scherette (Bö Jr.'s eldest daughter): "I remember the trips on my grandparents' yacht. They'd put us downstairs, and we'd watch Balboa pass by through the portholes, too excited to sleep. Then we would creep up the galley stairs to the pilothouse, sit on his great lap, and listen to him and the captain, and he would tell us about the bay and the yacht. Once we docked in Catalina, he would take me on shore for a walk, then we'd have an early lunch. He would eat the gristle and so would I. He drank the buttermilk and so would I. In town he loved to take us to the Luau in Beverly Hills. Just about everywhere he went, everyone knew him and treated him like royalty.

"I remember his smile and bear hugs. We would sit and watch Fred MacMurray's TV show while he dictated into his machine, gave us his attention, and still watched the show.

"We flew on the first jet to Mexico and found ourselves written up in the newspapers as their children, not grandchildren, because my grandparents looked so young.

"My high school organized a trip to Europe so I decided to go to Italy and study art history and Italian. My grandfather's good friend Monsignor Ragni took me on a private tour of the Vatican.

"We corresponded a lot over the years. People often said Grandfather had had a Horatio Alger life. This is what he advised me: 'I thank you for your sweet note and if you have a chance, drop me a line and tell me about your plan of life. It is so essential that you have a program of progression. Goals are important. All my life I have set up certain goals to attain; a few times I have failed but have had a good average, on successful moves. Planning your life is a great challenge and completing each phase of life with the satisfaction that you have done a good job is important.'"

My son **Denis Olsen**'s remembrances are in the "Fun & Frolic" chapter.

Shirley Patton (Dad's niece and the daughter of his brother Ed) wrote me: "I remember your dad with fond memories. He was part of our life from the beginning and to the end of his ... He was lots of fun as was my dad. They were so alike, ready to clown, have fun and laugh. They made growing up wonderful ... He would call on a weekend and tell my folks 'be ready. I'm coming by' and off we would go in any direction for a fun day ... If he saw a road and didn't know where it went, we would go on it ... As we grew older we were expected on Sundays. When we started dating, we brought the dates along for the day, too. Family was very important to him. We all sometimes worked part time for him at Beverly Management Corporation, and he expected us all to do a good job. When my dad got older and had health problems Uncle Bö would often visit for several hours on the weekends in Anaheim. He was good to the entire family—his nephew, his brothers and all of us kids ... I will always remember him with much love, and he gave love to many."

My brother wrote, "Dad was a friend to everyone he met and did many unselfish things over the years. I will always remember how he would back, financially, an out of work client or friend, and I don't remember his asking for anything in return. I think he knew that this movie business was so temporary that he couldn't say no. Everyone ended their stories with the sentiment about my father that John Wayne expressed at the funeral: "I loved that guy.""

* * * * *

My memories about my father:

As I said at the beginning, I knew I was "Daddy's Girl," and I was proud of it. It made me feel secure, a security that was lost when he died. I always knew that he was there in case of an emergency when my own resources were inadequate.

He was not the perfect father. He had a temper that I was lucky never to have directed at me. He joined many of the Hollywood gang by having extramarital affairs, and his business took him away from home quite a lot.

BUT—WE HAD FUN! Whether it was at home or on his boat in Catalina or at a nightclub in Hollywood or just being around him during the years I worked for him at Beverly Management Corporation. He loved Sundays and having people around him all the time and almost made it a command performance for the whole family (mine, my brother's, and my uncle Ed's) to show up.

It has been a joy to look back and remember so many of the good times and even some of the difficult times of my life with my father. As he said so many times in ending the hundreds of letters he wrote every year to family and his many friends all around the world, "Arms Around You." I always knew his arms were there, ready and waiting.

One day I was looking through Dad's desk drawers and came across a very old Christian Science Prayer Book. When we were young, my brother and I had attended a nearby Christian Science Sunday school until a good friend of my parents died of a burst appendix, having refused to call for medical help, and they quickly took us out of the Sunday school.

When I opened the prayer book, I found the inscription "Remember, I Shall Return" written on the cover page in my father's adult handwriting.

Over the years I've thought about what he meant by that. Did he mean it to be a religious inscription? I never thought of my parents as being particularly religious, but perhaps they were. My mother lived to be 95½, outliving Dad by twenty-six years. Her last words were "It is time for the angels to come and take me up," and they did within the hour. Maybe Dad had a spiritual side to him, too.

After Dad died in 1973, we were staying at the house in Catalina a lot. I often tossed all night with a very strange feeling coming over me. In talking with our friends Frank and Betty Buck, who had lived in our house while theirs was being built, they remarked that they had both felt a cold presence in the house, had seen a swirling fog, and that their dog refused to go upstairs. Various incidents happened such as smoke alarms, the radio, and lights going on and off for no reason. At times I would wake up feeling pressure on my body as I was sleeping, and I'd feel paralyzed, not able to move, as if something was trying to get into my body. It was so upsetting that we finally called Dr. Barry Taft, a parapsychologist at UCLA, who brought his team to investigate the phenomenon. They concluded that there were two spirits, not just one, in the house. Whatever it was, it finally left in peace ten years later in 1983.

I remember the night after Dad died I walked the floor most of the night thinking, Please be at peace. You have died and are on your way to your next life. You cannot come back. But he had written in his Christian Science Prayer Book, "Remember, I Shall Return." Did he mean he'd try to contact us? I don't know, but maybe he *has* returned in spirit in a way through this book that tells his story. Here's to you, Dad—remembered!

HERE'S TO YOU, DAD... REMEMBERED

CHAPTER 16

CAST OF CHARACTERS

*O*ver the years, Beverly Management Corporation handled the finances of more than 100 clients in various phases of their careers in the entertainment industry. Some were among the biggest names in Hollywood, and their stars burned bright and long. Many went on to develop their own production companies with their own business managers. Others passed quickly from view, never to be seen or heard from again. Others, like Fred MacMurray, were with us for years. Not everyone was memorable. I'd rather forget some of the most difficult. Some of their stories have already been told in previous chapters, but here are the clients I especially remember:

Rex Allen—The *Arizona Cowboy* was the last of Hollywood's singing cowboys, following Roy Rogers and Gene Autry's B Western movie trail at Republic Studios. He rode his horse Koko everywhere, including Las Vegas showrooms, our office, and the barbershop across the street. Neither he nor the horse needed a haircut, but it made for great publicity. He and his wife, Bonnie, spent every free moment at their ranch in the San Fernando Valley.

The Andrews Sisters—La Verne, Maxine, and Patty were known as "America's Wartime Sweethearts" and became one of the best-known groups in the Big Band era and for keeping up the morale of the troops during World War II.

James Arness was best known for his eighteen seasons as Marshal Matt Dillon on the TV classic *Gunsmoke*. Six foot six, he came to Hollywood as a veteran of World War II. *Celebrity Register* described him as follows: "A multi-millionaire from his income for his years on *Gunsmoke*, he divides his time between homes in Los Angeles and his 100 acre 'ranchette' in the hills near Santa Barbara."

John Barrymore—"The Great Profile" was a member of the legendary family of actors, which included Ethel and Lionel. When he came to Hollywood, we managed his finances for a while—as far as he was manageable. If there was a vice he didn't have—women, booze, drugs, debauchery, self-destructiveness—I don't know what it was. He was married to Dolores Costello, to whom Dad was close. Actress Drew Barrymore is the granddaughter of John and Dolores. *John Barrymore Jr.*—A member of the Barrymore theatrical dynasty, he found it hard to live up to his legacy. He was married to Cara Williams, another client.

Ward Bond was a teammate of John Wayne's on the USC football team when director John Ford hired them as extras for his 1929 silent movie *Salute*. They went on to make many movies together, including *The Quiet Man*, *She Wore a Yellow Ribbon*, and *The Searchers*. He was known as one of Hollywood's most outstanding character actors and was Officer Bert in the classic film *It's a Wonderful Life*. He starred as the wagon master in the NBC TV series *Wagon Train*. Ward was tight-fisted, conservative, tough, and smart. How smart? He married my dad's secretary Mary Lou May, who taught me so much. I worked toward her job and finally got it when she married Ward and stopped being a career girl. When Ward got into a motorcycle accident, Dad quickly called for help on his car phone (one of the few car phones of that time). Ward was rushed to the hospital, where the doctors wanted to amputate his leg. Dad stormed in, took over, wouldn't allow the amputation, and helped persuade the doctors to save Ward's leg.

Frank Borzage (pronounced Bor-ZAY-ghee) was a client for years. He won Academy Awards for silent and sound movies. He started as an actor and then became a director with *Humoresque* in 1920. He went on to direct outstanding actors such as Janet Gaynor, Charles Farrell, Helen Hayes, and Gary Cooper. His movies are considered old-fashioned by many except movie buffs who keep "rediscovering" his work.

George Brent was suave, tall, gallant, and dependable. During the Irish Rebellion he had to be smuggled out of Ireland for subversive activities. He landed in Hollywood in the late '20s and played opposite Bette Davis, Olivia de Havilland, Barbara Stanwyck, and many other top stars. He played Pat Denning in *42nd Street* with Ruby Keeler and portrayed King Richard the Lion-Hearted in *The Adventures of Robin Hood* with Errol Flynn. Like many of the leading men types I knew, he was married more than once (six times, I think) and retired to his ranch. Dad always promoted real estate!

Bruce Cabot saved Fay Wray from King Kong's clutches. After 1961 he worked mostly with his longtime buddy John Wayne on movies such as *The Green Berets*, *Chisum*, and *The Comancheros*. Known as a rugged, two-fisted guy, he came from a family of diplomats.

Rory Calhoun—Like a lot of actors, he started out with an unlikely name (Francis Durgin). He went from films to TV in the late 1950s with a series called *The Texan*. He was a fun, flirty guy and was married to Lita Baron, another client.

John Carroll was a good-looking leading man with a very good singing voice. He played many roles where he lost the girl.

Linda Christian—There have been many stories written about Dad's connection to Linda, including one that says he sponsored her education and another that says her middle name of Christian was inspired by his.

Mae Clarke—All stars want a memorable moment on-screen. Mae's was when Jimmy Cagney shoved a grapefruit in her face in *Public Enemy*. Her career peaked in the early 1930s, about the time Dad started the business.

Joan Crawford—*Yahoo! Movies* says Crawford "was not an actress, she was a movie star." She was one tough cookie, very demanding. Her long career, volatile personal life, and troubled relationship with her children have been chronicled many times, including a scathing biography called *Mommie Dearest*, written by her daughter.

Bebe Daniels—Several years before she and her husband, Ben Lyon, became Dad's first clients, Bebe had a colorful run-in with the law. A Jazz Age film star at the age of eighteen, she was caught speeding in Santa Ana at 56.25 miles an hour (20 mph over the limit) in her Marmon Roadster (a car also owned by F. Scott Fitzgerald). Hundreds of spectators came to the trial. At its conclusion, she told the judge, "I suppose 56.25 mph sounds awfully fast if you've never driven anything faster than a plow." Her ten-day jail stay turned into a circus for the press, her fans, and the 792 people who signed her guestbook. Local restaurants delivered three meals a day. Her jail cell had a fancy bed, a Victrola, and other comforts, and at night Abe Lyman and the Cocoanut Grove Orchestra serenaded her under her jailhouse window. It even led to her starring role in *The Speed Girl*, which was filmed at the courthouse where she was convicted.

Billy Daniels—Daniels was a well-known choreographer and good friend of my parents. He and his mother were often at the house for dinner.

Marlene Dietrich—She may have been our most glamorous and amorous client. Once Dad told me he might have to go to South America, where John Wayne and Dietrich were on location. Duke had called, asking him to bring down a white mink coat in Dietrich's size, so he assumed the two of them were "getting together." In her autobiography, Pilar Wayne says Duke and Marlene had a three-year-long love affair. True? Maria Riva, Dietrich's daughter, wrote in her biography *Marlene Dietrich*, "His (Duke's) refusal to become one of her (Dietrich's) many conquests absolutely infuriated her."

Edward Dmytryk directed such films as *Murder, My Sweet* and *Farewell, My Lovely* with Dick Powell, and *The Caine Mutiny*. One of the blacklisted Hollywood Ten in 1948, he moved to England but returned to the United States in 1951, becoming a friendly witness. His autobiography was titled *It's a Hell of a Life, But Not a Bad Living*, which I always thought was a neat title for a life in Hollywood.

Ann Dvorak—Dad and I were both crazy about her. I kept a bigger scrapbook on her than on any other client. She was talented and gorgeous. Howard Hughes put her under contract to play opposite Paul Muni in *Scarface*. I always thought she never went as far as she could have, probably because of her salary demands.

Talented and gorgeous women were a dime a dozen in those days.

Mark Evans became a big cheese on television as a producer, director, and writer. He lived in Dad's Malibu house, for a long time.

Bob Fellows was a director/producer and later partner to John Wayne. He and Dad both turned fifty at the same time, and we had the Century Party to celebrate.

Leslie Fenton was born in England but raised in the United States. He played the bootlegger in *The Public Enemy* in 1931 and became a director later with films such as *Whispering Smith*. He was married to Ann Dvorak, another client of ours. We had many husbands and wives on our client list, before, during, and after their marriages.

Nina Foch was a concert pianist and amateur painter before becoming an actress. She worked opposite Gene Kelly in *An American in Paris,* got a Best Supporting Actress nomination for *Executive Suite*, and has done a lot of work in TV. She was considered one of Hollywood's best acting coaches.

Gene Fowler was one of many writers we had as clients. He went on to direct and produce movies. A drinking buddy of Errol Flynn and John Barrymore, he was a close, very good friend of Red Skelton. His son, Will Fowler, is also a famous writer.

Jean Gabin was famous in French musical reviews, operettas, and with the Moulin Rouge before he came to Hollywood. Maria Riva, in her biography of her mother, *Marlene Dietrich,* writes, "Dietrich's arms were waiting, ready to enfold him ... All he had to do was surrender himself into her loving hands ... and one of the great romances of the 1940s was born." His demands at Twentieth Century Fox did not go over well. When they fired him and paid him off, he went back to join the French troops in North Africa. When he needed money, she helped him out.

Jan Garber and his band. Jan started his first band in 1918 and is credited with having good business sense, putting together one of the best jazz bands around in the late '20s, and with helping elevate bands to "big business status." He claimed to have been the inventor of the "one-night stand"—for bands, that is. On his first trip to the West Coast in 1934, he played the Avalon Ballroom on Catalina Island. After living on the West Coast for years, he moved to Louisiana, which was the hometown of his wife, Dorothy, and continued to tour. In 1959, the Ballroom Operators of America honored him as leading the "Number One All Around Dance Band."

John Gielgud was a client of ours before he was knighted by the Queen of England. He was known for his virtuoso performances in Shakespeare plays, as Dudley Moore's butler in *Arthur*, and on television miniseries such as *Brideshead Revisited*.

Kathryn Grayson is a coloratura soprano who was discovered as a teenager singing on Eddie Cantor's radio program. She starred in some of MGM's best musicals in the 1940s and 1950s opposite Gene Kelly, Frank Sinatra, and Mario Lanza. One of her best pairings was with baritone Howard Keel in *Showboat* and *Kiss Me, Kate*. Her ex-husband John Shelton, was another of our clients.

Jon Hall at his peak would have been known as a "hunk" nowadays for his pumped-up, beefy build. He was called "The King of Technicolor" and appeared in films such as *Arabian Nights* and *Sudan* with sultry Maria Montez and Dorothy Lamour in John Ford's *The Hurricane*. He is credited with inventing the panoramic camera. At one time he was married to another client, Frances Langford. Sadly, when he got a diagnosis of terminal bladder cancer, he committed suicide in 1979.

June Haver—She and her husband, Fred MacMurray, were dear to us for many years. Fred was a client before he met her. See Chapter 12 for more details.

Rita Hayworth was one of Hollywood's most famous glamour girls, whose husbands included an agent, a playboy (Aly Khan), a singer (Dick Haynes), a producer (James Hill), and a genius (Orson Welles).

John Howard usually shied away from publicity, but as a navy man, he capped the climax when he was a junior officer on a minesweeper, which was sunk during the invasion of southern France. The navy revealed the details when an admiral pinned the Navy Cross on him, making him one of Hollywood's real fighting heroes. The citation read, "For extraordinary heroism." They said that Howard took over when his superior officer was wounded, supervised the transfer of casualties from the sinking ship, and personally searched the vessel to see that no one was left. When one of the rescue ships hit a mine, he dived into the water to save a wounded member of his crew. John had a beautiful voice and appeared in light opera. He often sang at our parties, in the office, in the car, or wherever there was an audience. He played Detective Bulldog Drummond in seven B movies and became the star of the first filmed television series, *Public Prosecutor*, in 1947.

Ian Hunter served in World Wars I and II, sandwiched between playing in Hollywood films starting in 1923. His British accent served him well in more than one Shirley Temple movie, in Sherlock Holmes films, and in *Broadway Melody of 1940*. He was a very close friend of Mom and Dad's. He introduced Gene Raymond and Jeannette McDonald to them, and they became our clients as well as personal friends.

Rita Johnson was on Broadway in films starting in 1935 and was known for her versatility in films such as *My Friend Flicka* and *The Major and the Minor,* and opposite Robert Young in *They Won't Believe Me.* She had a tragic accident in 1938 that required brain surgery, and died of a brain hemorrhage.

Van Johnson always looked like the "boy next door" and was known for his blue eyes, red socks, and freckles. He told me he made his living from his freckles—a dollar a freckle. The bobbysoxers went wild for him, and he caused a real flurry when he came to the office. Exempted from the draft because of a serious injury he had suffered in a car crash, he arrived in Hollywood in 1941 and eventually signed with Metro Goldwyn Mayer, where he made more than 100 films. He and Keenan Wynn were close friends until Evie Wynn divorced Keenan and married Van. I hear he lives somewhere in the state of New York and still does regional theater.

Jennifer Jones was a client for a while, together with her then husband Robert Walker, whom she divorced to marry producer David O. Selznick in 1949. She was nominated for the Oscar for two of her films, *The Song of Bernadette* and *Love Is a Many Splendored Thing.* Among her other films was *A Duel in the Sun.*

Victor Jory made dozens of TV episodes and more than 150 films. *Yahoo! Movies* says, "He was also more than generous with young up-and-coming actors (except for self-involved method performers), and was a veritable fountain of Broadway and Hollywood anecdotes, some of which were actually true."

Howard Keel starred in many musicals at MGM, on stage, on Broadway, and with touring companies. He was a great hit in England, where he helped to raise thousands of dollars for charity. He also starred on TV in *Dallas* for what he called "twelve amazing years." He was a major player in the Golden Age of Hollywood Musicals, starring in *Annie Get Your Gun* with Betty Hutton, *Show Boat* with Kathryn Grayson, and his favorite, *Seven Brides for Seven Brothers*, with Jane Powell. His wife, Judy, says his first ambition was to be a concert singer. He passed away in 2004.

Edgar Kennedy claimed to be one of the original Keystone Cops, starting his career working for Mack Sennett in 1914. In the 1920s, he went to work for Hal Roach in Laurel & Hardy and Our Gang films. He was the lemonade vendor in the Marx Brothers' *Duck Soup*. Between 1931 and 1948 he made more than 103 of his own two-reel comedies for RKO while appearing in many supporting roles in full-length movies.

Patric Knowles was another British lover type who played supporting roles to actors such as Errol Flynn in *Charge of the Light Brigade* and as Mame's suitor in *Auntie Mame*. He didn't have a mean bone in his body and was one of The Old Shoes. Although he was quite a lady's man at one point, he was nevertheless devoted to his wife and took wonderful care of her when she became blind.

Dorothy Lamour—When Dorothy came to the office, she didn't wear a sarong, and she didn't bring along Bing Crosby and Bob Hope, her costars in the wildly successful Road pictures. She was a big hit on her USO tours during World War II. She gave me a special doll to put over my bed when my first husband came home from overseas to, as she put it, "help you get pregnant." It worked. Nine months later Denis was born.

Carole Landis was a client for a while who came to a tragic end at a young age.

Frances Langford was a band singer in the '30s who made her movie debut in 1935, flourished as Bob Hope's vocalist on his radio show, and toured with him entertaining troops during World War II. In films, she crooned songs such as "I'm in the Mood for Love" and "You Are My Lucky Star" and made comedy records with Don Ameche as the distaff side of the Battling Bickersons. She played herself in *The Glenn Miller Story*, released in 1954. At one time she was married to Jon Hall.

Peter Lawford was a jet setter, good looking, always broke, a hit with the ladies, a high liver, and a player. I knew him before he married Patricia Kennedy, which made him JFK's brother-in-law, and before he became a member of Sinatra's Rat Pack.

J. Mitchell Leisen—Mitch had a unique background as an architect and artist before he turned to designing sets and costumes for the movies. David Thomson in *A Biographical Dictionary of Film* credits Leisen as "the man most responsible for the lustrous look of Paramount films," such as *Robin Hood*, *Lady in the Dark* with Ginger Rogers, and *Golden Earrings* with Marlene Dietrich. Olivia de Havilland, who played Melanie in *Gone With the Wind* and starred opposite Errol Flynn in eight films, was interviewed by Kevin Thomas of the *Los Angeles Times* on the occasion of her ninetieth birthday. He reported that "she retains a fondness for ... Mitchell Leisen, who directed her ... in *To Each His Own* ... (and) *Hold Back the Dawn*." According to Thomas, "Both her films for Leisen are marked by fine shadings in the performances and a concern for nuance and telling detail." When the studio system collapsed, Mitch moved to television. He was a member of The Old Shoes. He had a long-term relationship with choreographer Billy Daniels.

William Lundigan started as a radio announcer and worked in the movies in the late 1930s and 1940s opposite actresses such as Susan Hayward, June Haver, and Jeanne Crain. In the 1950s and 1960s he hosted TV series such as *Climax, Shower of Stars*, and *Men Into Space*. He was an adorable alcoholic and one of my favorites.

Ben Lyon was Dad's first client with his wife, Bebe Daniels. They were married in 1930 with gossip columnist Louella Parsons, Bebe's friend, as maid of honor. At one time Ben was a casting director at Twentieth Century Fox, where, according to Sheilah Graham in *Hollywood Revisited*, he was having an affair with Marilyn Monroe.

Jeannette MacDonald had been a leading lady as a soprano in operettas and musical comedies on Broadway in the 1920s until Ernst Lubitsch brought her to Hollywood. She became a big hit in films such as *The Merry Widow* with Maurice Chevalier, *San Francisco* with Clark Gable, and numerous films with Nelson Eddy. She was a doll and would sing at my parents' parties. Her husband, Gene Raymond, was another client.

Andrew McLaglen's father was the famous actor Victor McLaglen. Scott Eyman in his biography of John Ford, *Print the Legend*, chronicles Andy's remembrances of working with Ford on *The Quiet Man* as his assistant director. "Pappy" Ford insisted that all cast members be in wardrobe and on the set every day whether they were scheduled to work or not, knowing how fickle the Irish weather was for outdoor location filming. Among Andy's other credits are directing *McLintock* and *Gunsmoke*.

Fred MacMurray was known as one of the wealthiest men in Hollywood. His family and ours were together quite often, and we still have some investments together. His first wife, Lillian, was also well loved by my folks and was very kind and gracious to me as a young teenager. Lillian always gave Fred a surprise birthday party and made someone keep him occupied beforehand so he'd be surprised.,,, Because it was an annual event,

Ray Milland was Welsh, not British. He spanned the Hollywood scene for years in films such as *Beau Geste, The Lost Weekend,* for which he won an Oscar, Alfred Hitchcock's *Dial M for Murder,* and *Love Story* in the 1970s. He also directed several feature films and starred in television series.

Robert Nathan was one of our writing clients, remembered especially for *Portrait of Jennie.*

Lloyd Nolan and his wife, Mel, were longtime clients. He portrayed the crabby Dr. Chegley on the Diahann Carroll sitcom *Julia* and the paranoid Captain Queeg in *The Caine Mutiny Court Martial.* He had a photographic memory as far as scripts were concerned but was forgetful about everything else, including how to get to his own house.

Merle Oberon was born in India to an Indian mother and an Indo-Irish father and came to England in 1928, where Alexander Korda discovered her and groomed her to be a star. In 1935 he sold shares in her contract to Samuel Goldwyn, who gave her the lead in *The Dark Angel,* for which she was nominated for an Oscar. She married Korda in 1939 and divorced him in 1945. Probably her best-remembered film was *Wuthering Heights* in 1939, in which she played opposite Laurence Olivier. I remember she slept on her back so she wouldn't get wrinkles. She passed her mother off as her maid, since there would have been some prejudice in those days about her being Indian. She invested in the Cabana Club and left quickly as a client after that folded.

Harriet Parsons was a client until BMC closed its doors. At one point, *Newsweek* magazine called her "Hollywood's lone active woman producer." Her film credits include *The Enchanted Cottage* with Robert Young, *Susan Slept Here*, and *I Remember Mama*. Her mother was famed gossip columnist Louella Parsons. Harriet was married briefly to actor/playwright King Kennedy in front of 400 guests. Reputedly, Louis B. Mayer postponed the premiere of the film *Elizabeth and Essex* at a cost of $10,000 so people could attend the wedding. They soon divorced, and he went to work as a legman for Louella's archrival, Hedda Hopper. Harriet and her longtime girlfriend were frequently at the poker parties at Mom and Dad's home.

Anthony Quinn had three mistresses (more or less), thirteen children, and two wives—but who's counting? He appeared in films for more than sixty years, won his first Oscar as Marlon Brando's brother in *Viva Zapata!*, and starred in films such as *Guns of Navarone, Zorba the Greek, La Strada*, and *Lawrence of Arabia*.

Martin Rackin was a young delivery boy when he met humorist Damon Runyon, who encouraged him to be a writer. He started as a copy boy for the *New York Mirror* in his teens and worked his way up to columnist while also working as a publicist and speechwriter. He moved to Hollywood in 1941 and became a screenwriter, writing for Red Skelton, and became Red's producer for the TV show in the 1950s. From 1960 to 1964 he was head of production at Paramount Studios and then became an independent producer. In 1972 he completed his final production, *Two Mules for Sister Sara*.

Gene Raymond was a client, as was his wife, Jeannette MacDonald. When she died in 1965, he started showing up on my mom's doorstep in time for dinner, uninvited, unannounced, but welcomed. He brought a lawsuit against BMC, which wasted a lot of money in legal fees. The lawsuit didn't stop him from showing up for dinner, night after night after night. We met him often for lunch at the Regency Beverly Wilshire Hotel.

David Rose was an orchestra leader and composer who was on Red Skelton's radio show and was the only regular on his television show for twenty years. Themes on the shows "Holiday for Strings," "Lovable Clown," and "Our Waltz" were all composed by David. He and his wife, Betty, were a devoted couple and good friends of my parents

George Seaton was for many years the president of the Motion Picture Academy. Seaton was a Hollywood contract writer at MGM starting in 1933. He won Oscars for the screenplays of *Miracle on 34th Street* (which he also directed), and *The Country Girl* (for which Grace Kelly won an Oscar), and was nominated for Oscars for *Airport* and *The Song of Bernadette*.

Red Skelton was one of our most important clients. We have a whole chapter on him and many other references throughout this book.

Colin Tapley won a talent contest to get to Hollywood. Born in New Zealand, he looked great in military uniforms in both American and English movies. He was introduced to us by Ian Hunter.

Phillip Terry was a client, as was his then wife, Joan Crawford.

Lupe Velez has an entire chapter devoted to her.

Robert Walker looked boyish and was charming, but supposedly he suffered from anxiety attacks and was institutionalized after a severe nervous breakdown. I never saw any evidence of his problems, which culminated in his death and are still a controversial topic. Some say it was suicide; others claim it was an accident caused by an overdose of medication by his doctors. He starred in films such as *See Here, Private Hargrove* and *Strangers on a Train* with Alfred Hitchcock. He was married to Jennifer Jones, who divorced him and married producer David O. Selznick.

John Wayne—Duke was special in our lives, and our complicated personal and business relationship is covered throughout the book.

Johnny Weissmuller—Our relationship was almost that of big brother and little sister. He was one of many clients for whom I handled fan mail, answering letters and signing photos with his "autograph." Lupe Velez was one of his wives.

Orson Welles—Hollywood's big genius. He was a client for a short time when he was married to Rita Hayworth, and was a member of The Old Shoes. He made Hollywood history and some bitter enemies with his movie *Citizen Kane*, based on media mogul William Randolph Hearst and his relationship with Marion Davies.

Henry Wilcoxson came to Hollywood from England to play Richard the Lion-Hearted in Cecil B. DeMille's *The Crusaders*. He went on to become DeMille's associate producer and right-hand man. He also played many character parts in films and guest-starred on television programs such as *Marcus Welby, M.D.*

Keenan Wynn was the son of comedian Ed Wynn. His biggest successes were in the 1960s and 1970s in Disney films such as *The*

Absent-Minded Professor and *The Love Bug* and in TV series such as *Dallas*. Wynn's and Van Johnson's paths crossed in unusual ways, including Evie Wynn divorcing Keenan and marrying Johnson, supposedly at the urging of movie mogul Louis B. Mayer.

The family and friends above may not have been famous movie stars, but they were important to the happiness of our lives. Sundays at the Roos' home found Grandmother and Grandfather Holmes in front at the far right and Dad and his brother Ed at the far left, with Bö, Jr., Mom and I with the cousins and aunts and uncles above. God bless them all.

Biographies & Autobiographies

Barbas, Samantha. *The First Lady of Hollywood*. University of
California Press, 2005.

Blackwell, Earl. *Celebrity Register*. Celebrity Register, 1986.

Christian, Linda. *Linda, My Own Story*. Crown Books, 1962.

Conner, Floyd. *Lupe Velez and Her Lovers*. Barricade Books,
1993.

Degregorio, William. *The Complete Book of U.S. Presidents*.
Wings Books, 1991.

Eyman, Scott. *Lion of Hollywood*. Simon & Schuster, 2005.

Fonteyn, Margot. *Margot Fonteyn Autobiography*. Warner Books,
1976.

Freedland, Michael. *The Two Lives of Errol Flynn*. Bantam, 1980.

Keel, Howard. *Only Make Believe*. Barricade, 2005.

Keyes, Evelyn. *I'll Think About That Tomorrow*. Dutton, 1991.

Marx, Arthur. "Red Skelton," excerpted in *The Enquirer.*

O'Hara, Maureen. *'Tis Herself.* Simon & Schuster, 2004.

Riva, Maria. *Marlene Dietrich.* Knopf, 1993.

Roberts, Randy, and James S. Olson. *John Wayne, American.* Free Press, 1955.

Rogers, Henry C. *Walking the Tightrope.* William Morrow, 1980.

Rosenthal, Lee. *Catalina in the Movies.* Windgate Press, 2003.

Sharp, Kathleen. *Mr. & Mrs. Hollywood.* Carroll & Graf, 2003.

Thomson, David. *A Biographical Dictionary of Film.* William Morrow, 1981.

Wayne, Aissa. *John Wayne, My Father.* Random House, 1991.

Wayne, Pilar. *John Wayne—My Life with the Duke.* McGraw Hill, 1987.

Weissmuller, Johnny Jr. with William Reed. *Tarzan, My Father.* ECW Press, 2002.

Wilkerson, Tichi, and Marcia Borie. *Hollywood Legends.* Tale Weaver Publishing, 1988.

Zolotow, Maurice. *Shooting Star—A Biography of John Wayne.* Simon & Schuster, 1974.

General Reference

World Book Encyclopedia, various editions.

History

American Chronicle: Seven Decades in American Life—1920–1989.

Lois Gordon and Alan Gordon, Crown Publishers, 1987.

Chronicle of the 20th Century. Clifton Daniel, editor, Chronicle Publications, 1988.

Hollywood

Bacon, James. *Hollywood Is a Four Letter Town.* Henry Regnery Company, 1976.

Burk, Margaret. *Are the Stars Out Tonight? The Story of the Famous Ambassador & Cocoanut Grove—Hollywood's Hotel.* Copyright Margaret Tante Burk, 1980.

Carroll, Carroll. *None of Your Business.* Cowles Book Company, 1970.

Colombo, John Roberts, ed. *Popcorn in Paradise.* Holt, Rinehart, Winston, 1979.

Goodman, Ezra. *The Fifty-Year Decline & Fall of Hollywood.* Simon & Schuster, 1961.

Graham, Sheilah. *A State of Heat.* Bantam Books, April 1973.

Jarski, Rosemarie. *Hollywood Wit.* Prion, 2000.

Lasky, Jesse L., Jr. *Whatever Happened to Hollywood?* Funk & Wagnalls, 1973.

Powdermaker, Hortense. *Hollywood: The Dream Factory—An Anthropologist Looks at the Movie-Makers.* Little, Brown, 1950.

St. Johns, Adela. *Love, Laughter, and Tears.* Doubleday, 1978.

Silvester, Christoper, editor. *The Grove Book of Hollywood.* Grove Press, 1998.

Sperling, Cass Warner & Miller, Cork. *Hollywood Be Thy Name.* Prima Publishing, 1994.

Wilk, Max. *The Wit & Wisdom of Hollywood.* Atheneum, 1971.

Movies

Maltin, Leonard. *Leonard Maltin's Classic Movie Guide.* Plume, 2005.

Maltin, Leonard. *Leonard Maltin's Movie Encyclopedia.* Dutton, 1994.

Music

Simon, George T. *The Big Bands.* MacMillan, 1967.

Walker, Leo. *The Big Band Almanac.* Vinewood Enterprises, 1978.

Television

Brooks, Tim, and Earle F. Marsh. *The Complete Directory to Prime Time Network and Cable TV Shows 1946–Present.* Ballantine, 1999.

Gelman, Morrie & Gene Accas. *The Best in Television: 50 Years of Emmys.* General Publishing Group, December 1998.

Kisseloff, Jeff. *The Box: An Oral History of Television 1920–1961.* Viking, 1995.

Settel, Irving. *A Pictorial History of Television.* Frederick Ungar Publishing, 1983.

Other

Oliver, Mike. *Mike Oliver's Acapulco.* Writers Club Press, 2001.

Numerous clips: *Daily Variety, Herald Examiner, the Los Angeles Times, Hollywood Reporter*, and others. *Saturday Evening Post, Liberty Magazine, Cosmopolitan*, and others.

Special thanks to the Pasadena Public Library's excellent librarians, who were invaluable in the research.

PHOTO CREDITS

Hollywood–Associated Photos

De Wan Studios

Ralph Forney, Photographer

Pacific News Pictures

Los Angeles Times

David Kovar

Laughead Photographers

A Hal Marty Photo

Bob Plunkett, R.S.

Twentieth Century Fox

INDEX

Pitt, Brad 23
Polar Pantry 121, 165
Portago, Marquis de 130
Porter, Cole 7, 91, 133
Powdermaker, Hortense 39, 252
Powell, William 203
Power, Tyrone 81, 130
Punting & Sailing Club 199
Purdom, Edmund 130

Q

Quinn, Anthony 244

R

Rackin, Martin 244
Raymond, Gene 133, 189, 197, 239,
    242, 244
Remarque, Erich Maria 96
Reyes, Carlos 71, 73, 74, 105, 221
Righteous Brothers 203
Rin Tin Tin 90
Rio, Dolores Del 76
Riva, Maria 179, 235, 236, 250
Roach, L.A. County supervisor 47,
    102
Roberts, Julia 23
Roberts, Rachel 99
Rogers, Henry 50, 51, 250
Rogers & Cowan 51
Romero, Pepe 70, 74
Roos, Arthur Carl Herman 55
Roos, Bö, Jr. 222
Roos, Bö Christian Edward 55
Roos, Gladys Landl (Billie) Holmes
    53, 55
Roos, Grandfather Chris 53
Roos, Grandmother 55
Roos, Heidi 66
Roos family tree 211, 225
Rose, Betty 84
Rose, David 84, 156, 245
Rosenthal, Jerome 110
Rosenthal, Lee 212, 250
Rowley & Associates 168

Rumple, Top Banana 167
Ruser Jewelers 133
Russell, Gail 111

S

S.S. *America* 85
Sands of Iwo Jima 13, 86, 87
Santa Monica Deauville Club 170
Santiago, Adolfo 74, 77
Saturday Evening Post 1, 23, 173,
    183, 185, 253
Scaramucci, Vince and June 209
Scherette, Vicki Roos 225
Schiller, Bob 35
Schulberg, Budd 81, 89
Schwarzenegger, Arnold 161, 166,
    172, 173
Scott, Hampton 111
Scott, Randolph 96
Screen Actors Guild 33, 50
Scripps Clinic 140
Seaton, George 171, 245
Seeds, Russell M. 149, 155
Selznick, David O. 23, 239, 246
Selznick, Lewis J. 62
Sharp, Kathleen 47, 197, 250
Shay, Mildred 62
Shearer, Lloyd 42, 49
Shephard, Otis, Wrigley Company
    Artist 6
Silvers, Phil 155, 167
Simon's Drive In 204, 205
Simpson, Jessica 43
Sinatra, Frank 194, 205, 237
Singleton, Penny 29
Skelton, Edna 38, 169, 171, 182, 183
Skelton, Georgia 85
Skelton, Red 1, 15, 17, 29, 34, 38, 47,
    84, 85, 87, 96, 131, 135, 142,
    144, 145, 149, 152, 156, 158,
    169, 171, 182, 183, 193, 201,
    207, 208, 236, 244, 245, 250
Skelton, Richard 141, 148, 223
Smith, Adam, *Wealth of Nations* 174
St. Johns, Adela Rogers 129, 130

ABOUT THE AUTHORS

CAROLYN ROOS OLSEN worked with her father at the Beverly Management Corporation for twenty years during his lifetime and during the closing of the business following his death. For ten years, she was an executive in charge of the Monsanto Exhibit in Disneyland and for many years, she wrote monthly book reviews and a travel column for the *Avalon Bay News* on Catalina Island. She is active in promoting the Orange County Performing Arts in Costa Mesa, Calif..

MARYLYN HUDSON is a contributing editor to *Orange Coast* magazine, a co-founder of Round Table West book and author program, a book reviewer and member of the National Book Critics Circle. She is the author of a humor book and has written for *Palm Springs Life* magazine, *Trump Shuttle In Flight Magazine*, *Petite*, and other publications. She holds a B.A. from UCLA.

DENIS OLSEN, Carolyn Olsen's son and Bö Roos' grandson, is a world class award-winning artist whose work includes fine art, backdrops for film, theater, commercials, television, and murals. A graduate of Choinard Art Institute, he attended the Sorbonne, and was on staff at CBS, Disney, MGM, Warner Brothers and Grosh. He and his mother collaborated on the book cover design.

Printed in the United States
111442LV00004B/154-171/P